ON
BEING
A LEADER

PAMBANA MASAME

Leadership is under the spotlight today ... and the picture we are seeing is often not a positive one. Are leaders of today not only failing to live up to what is required of them personally but also letting society down? Starting (and staying) a leader is an art and a science – this book explores that premise.

P O Bx 601 AAH Masa, Gaborone
Tel: 267 73612905

pmasame@gmail.com
www.pambanamasame.co.bw

Published by Corporate Intervention (Pty) Ltd
corporateintervention@gmail.com
+276 71612905

Edited and Proof read
Chris Voysey
Chris Voysey Communications
chris@chrisvoysey.com

First Edition

DEDICATIONS

This book is dedicated to my wife, two daughters and a son, who I hope will enjoy a world in which leadership is taken more seriously and carried out more selflessly and purposefully.

INTRODUCTION

In the republished article *The Evolution of Leadership,* leadership researcher, Keith Cox PhD stated, "the word 'leader' entered the English language around the year 1300 and the methodical study of leadership began over 600 years later in the 1930's" (Cox, 2011)

Since the dawn of the word, hundreds of definitions for leadership have been set down by both practitioners and researchers.

Evidently, defining leadership is no easy task and the number of definitions might be equivalent to the number of authors. Consequently, there is no universally accepted leadership definition or standard.

But there are certain elements that appear frequently in writings on leadership such as the potential to inspire, motivate, stimulate good leader-follower relationships and nurture goal direction.

I believe that leadership can be defined as a process of societal influence maximising the efforts of others towards achievement of a common goal.

The perennial desire for leadership skills development is constantly fed by writings on the topic but little or no emphasis is given on the importance of choosing a leadership development method that actually works. To nurture positive leadership skills this method is urgently needed.

To show the relationship between a faulty leadership development method and a proven, working method, one can use an early-days medicine analogy.

Early day medicine comprised potions, lotions and pills, all of which had a common characteristic: they were all bitter. The early days healers believed that if it smells and tastes bad, it must work.

This has been passed on over centuries to leadership skill development authors who publish unproven methods which have produced the kind of heavy-handed leadership which alienates followers and often leaves a very bitter taste in the mouth!

In contrast, this book contains strategies and methods that can empower you as a leader and equip you with the leadership skills you need to inspire and motivate people, stimulate healthy leader-follower relationships and nurture goal direction in your followers.

This has been ensured by conducting profound research on development strategies. An effective leadership development strategy must motivate the reader to be a leader. (Reichard & Johnson, 2011). This book focuses on this aspect.

I aim to achieve this through an understanding of self-awareness, advice to help you keep your eye on the goal, steps on building your likeability as well as the motivation for constantly striving to be a better leader.

Welcome to an effective leadership skills development book. From the bottom of my heart, I hope this book helps you in your efforts to become a better leader.

HOW TO USE THIS BOOK

I am proud to present this collection of knowledge to help grow your leadership thinking. However, it is more than just another theory book on a well-known topic. It is my sincere belief that by understanding, and practising, the contents of this book, you will augment your leadership skills.

As we know, practice makes perfect and the important approach for this book is to practice whatever makes sense to you in the goal of being a great leader. As you practice, you become better at what you do.

Whether you are a union/political leader, manager in a world-class organization, a chief executive officer in a global company, a student in charge of your peers, or holding any position requiring leadership skills, the contents of the next pages will cast light on key skills and concepts that each and every leader should master.

In this book, you will learn what defines a leader, how to be a moral leader, how to lead with humility and much, much more.

Practice what you learn and become the kind of leader this world needs.

CONTENTS

SELF AWARENESS

This chapter is the starting point of the book and it is right that it should focus on the starting point of leadership (or any other self-development process):

Self-awareness.

Knowledge begins with knowing yourself and being true to yourself. This is particularly important to those who would be leaders.

Chapter one equips the reader with well researched information about self-awareness that is essential for handling the challenges that come with leadership.

The journey to self-awareness has been made easier by breaking down the major aspects of self-awareness: internal and external self-awareness, as well as simple steps on emotional awareness which are also included.

WHAT IS SELF AWARENESS?

Self-awareness is the ability to understand your strengths, weaknesses, emotions, needs, and motivations. It demarcates the difference between an excellent leader and a weak one.

Take, for instance, a leader who acknowledges his/her listening weakness and works on it actively without judging him or herself. With time, this leader will work through his or her vulnerability, develop active listening skills and earn the right to be referred to as a good leader.

A leader without self-awareness, however, would not work on the foible and would in consequence carry it through their lives and be a weaker leader as a result. The secret is, to be honest with yourself and others, and realize that the practice of self-awareness is the very thing that will strengthen and grow personal areas that require development.

Self-awareness is vital to a leader's comprehension of their goals and ethics (Goleman, 2019). To lead, one needs to know where one is headed and why.

Self-awareness tends to create a ripple effect of benefits. For example, a self-aware leader employing a task force will conduct interviews fairly and employ only the candidates best suited for the job, so that the task has the best chance of being done to the highest standard.

By doing this, the leader escapes the common problem found in workplaces, of incompetent employees who are not equipped for the job. By selecting the right people for the job, the leader can enjoy directing the task force and expect the best result.

From this, it is clear that mastering self-awareness has unpredictable positive upshots. The decisions made by self-aware leaders can benefit them in more ways than one.

Am I self-aware?

This is probably the question you're asking yourself as you read through this. In fact, it is the question you should be asking yourself!

Self-awareness is not a difficult characteristic to recognize. It shows itself directly through one's ability to gauge oneself sensibly. Self-aware leaders will always have the confidence to talk about their feelings about work openly and accurately.

Take a president of a country with low regard for civil rights, for instance. Although the public might be on tenterhooks waiting for a leader to address the issue, they need the motivation to be fully on board with the idea. By giving a simple but well-articulated speech that honestly addresses the important issue without trying to avoid it, the hearts and minds of the public will be won.

Those unaware of the issue will be made aware, and the leader will be one step closer to achieving his or her goals.

Admitting to failure is also a way to know if you are self-aware. The basic human understanding of a person who makes mistakes is that the person is weak. However, the reality is that any human being can make a mistake and on scrutiny, one can learn that once the person admits and rectifies the mistake, they no longer look weak but stronger. We can all identify with an acknowledgement of a mistake because we have all had the experience of making a mistake at some point or another.

The person who says 'we have made a mistake and we need to rectify it' is a much stronger human than the person who refuses to admit that a mistake has been made. By not dealing with the mistake, other mistakes are added and a compound effect creates potential chaos.

Admitting to mistakes gives way to learning from them while improving trust between the person and their followers. It also reveals the integrity of the person. More so, a leader is expected to take responsibility for mistakes on behalf of his/her followers, this builds trust (Eurich, 2019).

However, some moments even admitting to mistakes will not help a leader look stronger. If that leader constantly makes mistakes and does no more than admit to them, an impression of complete recklessness is given. It is vital for planning before acting so that mistakes can be avoided in the first place. That in itself, is a leader's responsibility.

Self-awareness can also be determined by performance reviews. A performance review is a formal assessment of performance, identifying the strengths and weaknesses of an individual which then offers feedback on the results.

This helps individuals comprehend what they are doing right and how to rectify what they are not doing right.

A self-aware leader needs to know his/her strengths and limitations to grow and develop into a better leader. The antithesis between a self-aware leader and one who is not is that the latter regards a correction as a threat or as an indication of failure as opposed to an opportunity to correct and learn from the error.

Self-confidence goes hand in hand with self-aware people. A point of view about your competencies is required especially for a person in leadership. It helps the leader accept himself and trust in himself. It asserts a sense of control in the leader's life.

With this, the leader can guide the followers more effectively by setting pragmatic goals and having realistic expectations. On the other hand, substandard self-confidence might make a leader feel submissive, willing to conform to the will of others in such a way that he or she avoids taking personal responsibility.

This can be seen as a toxic trait for a leader since that leader is expected to be the primary decision-maker. It is important to have a high perception of yourself even when dealing with low-ability problems.

Dale Carnegie once said that most of the important things in the world have been accomplished by people who have kept on trying when there seemed to be no hope at all. By this example, as a leader, you work on knowing yourself, identifying and developing the necessary skills and then mastering the self-confidence that comes with achievement of those personal goals.

CULTIVATING SELF AWARENESS

This chapter focuses on the 'how' of self-awareness. We have been talking about it but how do we do it? This is an important question – as we strive to develop skills, we need to get advice and pointers on how to do so.

Research shows that when we are more aware of ourselves, we feel more creative and confident (Spector, 2019). We set realistic goals and make sound and timely decisions as well as improve on our communication.

This is a skill many people aspire to possess but not many are willing to go through the process of development. The journey of learning how to cultivate self-awareness led to seven tips that can be used in its cultivation.

Self-awareness can be categorized into two main aspects:

Internal self-awareness, how we perceive our aspirations, zeal, principles, strengths, weaknesses, thoughts, and feelings.

External self-awareness, how other people see us.

The following tips will help empower both internal and external self-awareness

1. Focus on yourself

This requires mindfulness and focus. Meditation helps us to look at what might need to be worked on and developed.

Meditation happens when an individual practices mindfulness by focusing on a particular activity or thought to gain awareness and gain attention of oneself (Chopra, 2020).

Meditation is directly linked with self-awareness. This is because, through meditation, one is able to be fully aware of one's emotions, feelings, and environmental factors.

Negative feelings in particular are acknowledged by meditation. Through meditating, one can face up to and deal with feelings without simply avoiding them.

A leader must be able to deal with negative emotions to be freed to make better decisions. This is an important tool in mastering internal self-awareness.

2. Critique from friends and workmates.

No matter how frequently one might meditate, there are certain aspects of oneself that might be missed entirely unless they are pointed out by others.

Other people who know us can help us to know ourselves better. This is not always easy or comfortable and it is really important to be able to trust the people who you approach for feedback.

But the reality remains that the fastest and most effective way to find these aspects out is to ask for critique from those close to you.

Find a group of people who know a lot about you, and who's opinion you really trust and ask them for their honest opinion about you. The responses might be unexpected, but finding out the characteristics about yourself that you might have not noticed will help improve your external self-awareness.

3. Keeping a Journal

Keeping a regular record of your day-to-day tasks can be a great development tool for your state of mind. It is similar to meditation as it helps you to focus on behaviour and thought processes.

Contrary to popular belief, a journal is not only for the younger generation. It is a cardinal tool for keeping track of happenings in any leader's life and aids reflection into past decisions and processes.

To boost self-awareness through keeping a journal; write down notable events of the day, difficult decisions made and the different paths you could have taken, and confrontations with workmates and how you handled them.

Make sure to analyze your journal frequently to make the most out of it. This helps master internal self-awareness

4. Ask for advice

Gaining different perspectives is crucial for a person in leadership. It is very limiting to have only your own perspective on any particular issue. This is not a sign of weakness (no one person can have all the answers) – some of the greatest leaders of the world have had a strong advisory council to keep them abreast of activities.

A leader should intentionally get feedback from others by asking frequently from either superiors or advisors.

Nevertheless, not all advice should be taken. Learn to filter out advice and feedback that is not valuable. Conducting a 360-degree critique in the working place is an essential tool that improves a manager's self-awareness (Spector, 2019)

5. Listen

A good leader is almost always required to be a good communicator. The problem with frequent communicators is that they rarely sit back and listen.

There is a saying that God gave us two ears and one mouth so that we would listen twice as much as we speak. This is good advice for leaders.

To be a self-aware leader, it is essential to be a good listener. Listening helps create a connection with others as well as helps you to understand the needs of others.

When a leader masters the art of understanding the needs and lives of others, they can confidently say they are on the road to self-awareness. Listening gives way to numerous learning opportunities.

6. Spend time with others

It might surprise you how big an impact spending time with others can make on any human's life.

From birth, humans need to have someone, preferably more experienced in life, to mirror. When mirroring, one person unknowingly imitates another. This impacts directly on the lives of the two individuals.

Find yourself a mentor, someone you see as being self-aware from what you've gathered about self-awareness. Spending time with this person will greatly increase your self-awareness development chance.

It is also very important to get opinions different to your own so that you develop a rounded view. Spending time with people who think differently to you can help you hone and sharpen your own viewpoint, and certainly helps you to understand how other people think and feel.

7. Set realistic goals

Setting goals, realistic goals, is a skill that every leader should master. Not only should a good leader maintain goals, he/she should also keep track of the goals to determine how close he/she is to attaining them.

This has been proven to increase self-awareness (Spector, 2019).

The **S.M.A.R.T**. goals system is well-known and useful to bear in mind when setting goals and moving towards getting them realised:

S: **Specific** – generalised goals are difficult to follow. One needs to be as specific as possible when setting the goals.

M: **Measurable** – goals need to be measured and monitored so that one is motivated by knows how close one is to achieving them.

A: **Attainable** – if a goal is so far removed from achievement it simply de-motivates someone trying it achieve it.

R: **Realistic** – you need to know what you (and your team) are capable of; can you really achieve the goal you have set?

T: **Timely** – give yourself a manageable deadline; you cannot keep in pushing towards a goal that might be achieved 'some day'. When?

CHAPTER THREE

LEADERSHIP AND SELF AWARENESS ARCHETYPES

Tasha Eurich, Principal of the Eurich Group (and highly sought-after speaker on Leadership and developer of leadership tools) researched the two categories of self-awareness and came up with four self-awareness leadership archetypes which offer an important resource for understanding Self Awareness in Leadership.

Figure *1.0*

The four self-awareness archetypes.

	Low external self-awareness	High external self-awareness
High internal self-awareness	**INTROSPECTORS** They're clear on who they are but don't challenge their own views or search for blind spots by getting feedback from others. This can harm their relationships and limit their success.	**AWARE** They know who they are, what they want to accomplish, and seek out and value others' opinions. This is where leaders begin to fully realize the true benefits of self-awareness.
Low internal self-awareness	**SEEKERS** They don't yet know who they are, what they stand for, or how their teams see them. As a result, they might feel stuck or frustrated with their performance and relationships.	**PLEASERS** They can be so focused on appearing a certain way to others that they could be overlooking what matters to them. Over time, they tend to make choices that aren't in service of their own success and fulfillment.

Note. Adapted from 'What Self-Awareness Really Is (and How to cultivate it)' by T.Eurich, 2019, *Self-Awareness,* p.20. Copyright 2019 Harvard Business School Publishing Corporation.

A common mistake made by leaders is to focus on one category to the exclusion of others.

As you view these archetypes, I am sure you have will evaluate yourself in an attempt to see where you lie among the four archetypes. Placing yourself according to these categories also helps you to know what you need to change and/or develop to be more self-aware and more 'other-aware'.

AWARE

Obviously, the highest level of self-awareness is the 'Aware' category. In this category, the leader knows himself or herself very well and has a clear picture as well as how other people see him/her. Once mastering this level of Self Awareness – which is no easy task - a leader can truly reap the benefits of self-awareness.

The 'aware' leader has a rare balance between knowing him or herself and the people around them. He or she can understand that he has his own needs but is fully aware that the other also has need that must be met. A rare individual but so important that we can aspire to be that kind of leader.

INTROSPECTORS

'Introspectors' are those leaders who have mastered internal self-awareness. They are knowledgeable about their desires, feelings, goals, and purpose in life but have not taken the chance to find out how the outside world thinks about them.

The value of this category is in mastering true self-awareness. But to develop a greater awareness of how others see you, the best thing you can do is approach close friends and workmates and find out their honest opinion about you.

In this regard, the 4-step process below can act as a guide and help you to understand how people see you in the workplace.

It also offers you really important information that can help you develop a more favourable persona if that is what you need to do. And most leaders do need to do that!

SEEKER

The third archetype is the 'seeker' category. This is a common category for leaders who have not placed importance on self-awareness or the importance of knowing others.

This is a vulnerable category to be in and any leader who might find themselves in this group should aspire urgently to learn self-awareness – become more aware of themselves and where their weaknesses lie so that they can turn those weaknesses into strengths.

If you find yourself in this category, follow the seven steps of cultivating self-awareness referred to earlier in this book, sit back, and watch the magic happen.

PLEASERS

The final archetype, the 'pleasers', describes a leader who is focused on what other people think of him/her to the exclusion of understanding themselves.

The leader cares less about his/her goals, feelings, or motivations and the followers are the primary motivators.

This category has advantages and fits fairly well with the concept of the servant leader: however the danger is the leader becoming simply a puppet, which is not the purpose of servant leadership at all.

The servant leader - who is definitely there to serve his or her follows also has a very clear vision of what needs to be achieved and can lead his followers towards that objective knowing that it is a goal that is designed to suit everybody.

There is a persistent need to master internal self-awareness. Make choices you are comfortable with and your workplace will turn into your dream workplace. Remember, self-awareness is a delicate balance, without mastering both internal and external self-awareness, you cannot be the best version of yourself.

Feedback plays a very important role in Knowing oneself and Knowing Others. It is a true and brave leader who can find the mentors and colleagues in his workplace and encourage them to help him know himself better.

The model below can help in this important quest.

STEP 1

- Choose 5 trusted workmates, specifically those who see you often in the work setting.
- Ensure you have at least one influential workmate who might know more than you expect.
- Also be sure that these colleagues will tell you things honestly and openly

STEP 2

- Meet them physically and individually. Face-to-face encourages honesty and can be a mechanism of ensuring truth.
- Assure confidentiality - to inspire honesty and create a relationship of trust.

STEP 3

- Ask what general perception they have of you. Also ask for specifics - how you afffect them.
- Be sure not to ask 'guided' questions to hear what you want to hear.
- Ask what they think you can do to improve who you are and how you interact.

STEP 4

- If you receive negative information (or what you see as negative), try as hard as possible to contain your reaction.
- It is really important to see the truth of how you come across and reacting without umbrage will help your colleagues to be more honest with you with feedback.

MASTERING EMOTIONS

I t is not that long ago that a leader (or potential leader) would be measured mainly by IQ and intellectual knowledge of his or her subject.

Of course, there is no doubt that IQ (Intelligence Quotient) and knowledge will always be extremely important in a leader – the ability to use one's brain and mental capacity is crucial in leadership positions – but as the world has changed and people's expectations of leadership have shifted it is absolutely essential that a leader can be seen to exhibit Emotional Intelligence (EQ) as well.

This ability ensures that people feel that they are understood and cared for as humans, not just numbers in the voting game or pawns on the board of life.

Individual performance, productivity in the workplace, and the ability to motivate and develop people are essential skills a leader must have. These are directly affected by the leader's emotional intelligence (Serrat, 2009).

Emotional intelligence can be described as the self-perceived capacity to identify, assess, and manage sentiments about oneself, others, or a group. Emotional intelligence has been recently recognized as an important trait in choosing leaders.

In Chapter 4, I will be unpacking this new understanding of leadership capability showing the importance of emotional intelligence, understanding what it is and how one can master emotions to gain higher emotional intelligence and the ability to understand and lead people.

Understanding Emotions

In earlier chapters we discussed the importance of Self-Awareness and we see now that this can be further broken down into emotional awareness, accurate self-assessment, and self-confidence.

Leaders with high emotional awareness can learn from their feelings and exhibit an increased emotion control than those who don't. For instance, if the emotionally aware leader is feeling angry, he/she reflects on the feeling, finding out in the process what triggered the emotion and acts on it.

This is a far better reaction than expressing anger indiscriminately and alienating (even creating enemies out of) the people you work with. A sane and respected leader leads the workforce better far better than one who has no control over his or her emotions and reactions.

Through developing EQ, emotional intelligence, a leader is able to win people over, increase productivity and elevate the chances of success in projects. Stress levels in the workplace are also significantly reduced.

Have you ever worked in an environment where everyone seems to be passively or actively aggressive? Or in a place where everyone is under visible pressure from loads of work being thrown at them by a superior workmate? The feeling is not pleasant, the levels of trust are very low and people are not naturally productive but feel forced to comply as a result of pressure from above.

However, if the leader has mastered emotional awareness and the ability to control his/her feelings effectively, the results will be a calm working environment full of happy workers.

As a leader, it is essential to understand that feelings and emotions can directly (or indirectly) affect the mood, state-of-mind and performance ability of others.

The leader who has a clear concept of the wisdom of knowing and gaining control of the role of emotional awareness in their surroundings will foster stability and harmony in the workplace.

Predominately, the office is no place to bring non-work-related thoughts and feelings. However, while this might be decidedly true, it is completely against basic biology for any human to have an on and off switch for feelings. Human beings are emotional animals and very often make decisions based more on their emotional state than their intellectual one.

Those in executive positions, the leaders especially, are expected to be neutral with their feelings while in the office. They are expected to be appreciative of work done well and quick to give guidance for work done poorly.

It is essential for leaders to have a system of concealing and managing their own negative feelings while at work.

If you can identify with what is being said here, I presume you have a system for manging your emotions. Whether you use positive affirmations, drown yourself in work or even save up the negative feelings for later to focus on work without negative emotions, it is absolutely critical to give energy and attention to mastering emotional awareness.

In this next section we look at how we can deal with the powerful aspect of emotions in life.

Dealing with emotions

Instead of masking your emotions, as a leader, you should face them head-on mindfully and productively.

A phenomenon exists (The Ironic rebound) where if a group is told not to think of white bears, they might actually be more likely to think about it (Dostoevsky, 1863) If you try to suppress a thought, the thought might surface even more than if you were not trying to think about it. So it is with emotions.

Instead of deliberately suppressing emotions and thought, it is far more productive to be doing something about those emotions and using them to work for better not worse.

A system that has been shown to be very useful for this is the Acceptance and Commitment Therapy (ACT) developed by a psychologist at the University of Nevada, Stephen C. Hayes. The ACT therapy is broken down into four steps: Recognize your patterns, label your feelings and thoughts, accept the emotions, and act on values.

Step 1: Recognising patterns

In *Recognizing Patterns*, you should be able to notice when a feeling, thought, or emotion has become too powerful.

This can be done by checking to see if a thought, feeling, or emotion has become overly repetitive. Take for instance, when you've given an order to your follower and it is completed but not within the specifications needed, and you feel just a little irritated. The irritation, however, doesn't stop and continues for a few more hours or even the whole day like a broken record. Even when you've managed to brush the feeling off, just a little thing could trigger you into thinking of it. Recognition of the feeling is the first step in dealing with it.

Step 2: Labelling thoughts and feelings

When your mind is teeming with thoughts, you have to consider *Labeling these Thoughts*. This is where one needs to visualize the feeling either by saying the feeling to yourself or by writing it. For example, if feeling irritated like the example above, you can choose to say *I am having the thought that what my workmate did was not right, and that irritates me*. This will help you reflect on your feeling and see the feeling for what it is.

Research shows that humans are able to mentally picture personal experiences to ease the solving process. Doing this not only enhances behavior but also changes the behavioral functions of the brain (Eurich, 2019). It improves the emotional intelligence of the individual.

Step 3: Acceptance

The next stage after this is *acceptance.* This involves the acknowledgment of the thoughts and emotions and responding to them while still maintaining a positive outlook towards the experience of them.

It is by accepting emotions that we can move past them. During this period, as a leader, you should not judge yourself. Instead, you should be lenient with yourself and try to understand the situation better. Rather than taking out your emotion on others, take the time to notice that the emotion might be tied to your dedication to your work. There is nothing wrong with that dedication but it is important to realise that not all people might have the same level of dedication.

The other question to ask yourself is whether the instructions related to the task performed were clear for the individual performing them. If not, it would help to put energy into solving how instructions and communication could be improved.

In other words, one is looking at the issue from more than one perspective, dissolving the emotion and looking for a solution, rather than just reprimanding or creating ill feeling all round.

This will motivate you to work harder and be more productive. If the irritated leader referred to above, started yelling commands at everyone instead of clearly giving orders and requests, the workflow would turn out to be laggard. Accepting the feeling would make him a better leader.

Step 4: Acting on your values

The final stage is *acting on your values* - responding to the emotions in a way that corresponds with your values. If the values that you wish to have as a leader (and to be reflected in your workplace) are to be a clear communicator, have personnel that respect you, show respect for others, encourage understanding and right action, this situation gives you the opportunity to act accordingly.

After evaluating yourself thoroughly, find the best way to deal with the situation you're in. The solution should create positive effects for the organization.

In summary, it is incredibly difficult to brush off strong emotions and thoughts, Instead, an effective leader should face the thoughts and emotions head-on and look for a positive way to deal with them. Hurriedly finding a solution might hinder you from making the right choice. So, take your time when dealing with emotions.

Summary

Overall, as leaders, you need to be aware of your senses. Self-awareness will help you track your strengths, weaknesses, emotions, needs, and motivations.

- With self-awareness, a leader can acquire his/her true potential.

- There are two categories of self-awareness: internal and external self-awareness. Additionally, you must find the perfect balance of these to achieve complete self-awareness

- Self-awareness can be enhanced by following the seven tips: set realistic goals, meditation, asking for critique from friends and workmates, keeping a journal, asking for advice, listening, and spending time with others.

- Emotions should not be suppressed, instead, they should be faced head-on and dealt with to yield maximum results in the workplace

- Leaders with high emotional awareness can learn from their feelings and have increased emotion control than those with low emotional awareness.

- The four steps to dealing with emotions: Recognize your patterns, label your thoughts, Accept emotions and Act on your Values.

CHAPTER FIVE

CONNECTING WITH FOLLOWERS

The main aim of this chapter is to equip you with all the necessary tips and tricks you need to ensure you attract the required employee loyalty and trust that all leaders need to be successful in their particular fields.

As a leader, these skills are mandatory and surviving your leadership post is virtually impossible without them.

The chapter illustrates the different types of followers and it breaks down aspects one needs to pay attention to in ensuring that a connection between leader and follower is established and works in the most effective way possible.

Whether self-proclaimed, elected, or delegated, every leader will have a group of followers that he or she leads or commands. Understanding the follower will often come instinctively to an experienced leader but it is also an acquired skill to new and upcoming leaders.

However, if wise, both the new and the established leader will look more into the topic of connecting to leaders since it forms such an important part of being a successful leader.

Followers significantly influence leaders and the leadership process. After all, one cannot be a leader without people to lead. Successful leaders are defined by their traits and ability to understand and connect with their followers. But this should not be taken for granted as there is a wide range of followers' personality types, regardless of whether you have a high or low following.

Of course, based on your shrewd decision to read this book, I can already see how much easier it will be for you to develop a secure understanding and connection to your followers.

Juts before we dive into how to develop a connection with your followers, we must first understand the different types of followers you have encountered or might encounter in the future as a leader. Common mistakes leaders make is thinking of followers and employees as a single task force with similar needs.

Humans are defined by their physical features, language, ethnicity, and various traits, which gives a considerable allowance for diversity.

The three defining characteristics above are interesting but could be said to have a lower impact on leadership than the personal traits. Just as humans have a variety of personal characteristics, you will obviously meet followers with varying traits. Accepting the difference in traits among your followers will help your understanding of people and ensure an efficacious connection to your followers.

In this section, we will tackle the different types of followers that leaders are predestined to encounter in the wide field of leadership.

Types of Followers

Listed below are the types of followers I amassed from research and also who I personally encountered in my experience in leadership in the Central Executive Committee. This was the main governing body of the trade union, made up of office bearers elected at a National General Congress, a delegate gathering of members.

i) The Fawner

The allocated synonyms best describe the definition of this type of follower in the workplace as a *Yes-man, boot licker*. The odds of encountering a fawner in the workplace are similar to the reply you would give if someone randomly asked how you are doing. In other words, extremely high.

The fawners will try their level best to please the person in command, sometimes at the expense of themselves and their workmates. The fawners seem the easiest to control (since what pleases you, their leader, pleases them) but the never-ending flattery will retard a proud leader's path to success. They seldom give suggestions or raise concerns against what might be an inaccurate order received.

ii) The Realist

This type of follower takes situations seriously and is ready to accept and deal with any situation. Their mentality is that of grabbing the bull by its horns. They are known for their critical thinking toward essential matters and will freely suggest courses of action they feel should be taken to the leader if given a chance.

Having this type of follower can significantly improve the leader's path to success or destroy it. Once the realist disagrees with the leader's choices and methods, they are ready to change leadership.

iii) The Dutiful

Also known as the loyal. As the name suggests, they are the followers who remain conscientious and obedient to the leader. Being the most reliable to the leader, they are generally relatively hard working. This trait ensures they provide constant suggestions to the leader.

It could be said that a distinction exists between the dutiful and the realist in that the dutiful follower is satisfied with the leader's methods and choices whereas the realist can disagree and might not compromise.

iv) The Opportunist

This follower comes with a price tag. They are the followers that can easily be bought out, mostly following the leader that best benefits the follower. Opportunists abandon causes as soon as better causes arise, often abandoning a person in leadership once their influence is incapacitated.

Famous for their low regard for principles and planning, they pounce on the best opportunity. This trait brands them as low-trust followers. The leader is forced to be in constant contact with them, assuring their loyalty. Failure to do so can result in their desertion.

Being eloquent and compelling is a bonus in maintaining the support of these followers.

v) The Antagonist

Criticism as a leader is inescapable. It comes with the territory - not everyone is going to agree with your ideas or even your style of leadership. However, the type of follower mentioned in this section takes disagreeing to new levels as it is guaranteed that they are actively waiting on the slightest mistake you make.

Their point of sight is constantly challenging the one in command's behaviour and policies. With a variety in motif, ranging from losing an election or being denied a pay raise to missing a promotion, the antagonist is the most likely to challenge the one in leadership for the post.

vi) The Renegade

This is the most challenging follower to identify since they are generally the owners of a startling poker face. You can simply never be sure what they are believing.

They are the best in deception and might camouflage themselves as the dutiful, often laying down their guard when it is too late for the leader to see their true colours. They silently are against the leader, and keeping an eye out for them is crucial. They can be likened to a parasite that devours the host from the inside.

vii) The Onlooker

This type of follower might present themselves as shy or incompetent since they only watch from the side-lines. They do not participate but are more part of the audience and it must be said that the influence they have on the leader and the task force is of little consequence.

Working with the work-for-pay mentality, they do not go out of their way to provide suggestions for challenges encountered at the workplace and will scarcely influence the leader's choices and methods.

In conclusion to this section on types of flowers, it must be said that understanding who your followers are is vital to providing consistent results as a leader.

The biggest mistake you can make when establishing a connection with followers is to see them as a single task force. Learning and mastering an understanding of the different types of followers puts you at distinct advantage along the path of connecting with your followers.

A leader must employ different strategies that work for the different types of followers to connect effectively with the various types of followers who exist.

How to connect with your followers.

Effectively connecting with followers is not an easy task, and leaders must invest their time and resources to master the art. The tips described below will help you in your journey

Humans are known for their social nature, but no matter how social a person is, they cannot get along with everyone since they have different needs, wants, and beliefs.

This is obviously just as true of the people we call followers – they also have different needs and wants. This requires the leader to find a way as far as possible to satisfy the whole group if they plan to form a connection with their followers.

Of course, forming this connection can prove difficult (considering distinct characteristics and personalities, but, as a leader, you have to make relations with all your followers work somehow. To do this, an analysis of your followers is essential. You have to implement strategies that will leave all the different categories in your follower list satisfied.

Analyzing followers and employees gets more difficult as the size of your following increases. A leader with only a few followers will appropriately categorize them, but analysis for a leader with significant numbers of followers can prove difficult. The leader in such a situation must use his/her wits to approximate the range in categories of followers and put in place a strategy that does not favour any particular group but remains neutral to the different types of followers the leader will encounter.

Consider the 'Realist' and the 'Fawner' mentioned in the section above categorising types of followers: While the latter might be easier to please, the realist needs to see a leader who is prepared to listen and implements ideas.

In order to connect with both types of followers, the leader might be required to pay more attention to the needs of the realist since the fawner is already, by nature, willing to follow the leader's decision. In an attempt to acknowledge both types, an increase in the odds of forming a connection is realised.

Servant Leadership.

In the light of some heavy-handed, dictatorial leadership in world affairs, much has been written in the past years about the concept of Servant Leadership and this can be seen as a very effective way to interact with followers of all types.

Servant Leadership is a philosophy whereby the leader's goal is to engage in really understanding the needs of followers and to serve employees and followers by bringing these needs and wants to the forefront, aiming to connect at a very real level with followers and by this connection, enable employees to improve their performance (Sendjaya & Sarros, 2002).

This type of leadership ensures maximum interaction between leaders and their employees, providing endless bonding opportunities while simultaneously increasing the leader's likeability to the followers. Embracing the concept of servant leadership will significantly help with inspiring followership and connecting with your followers.

Being a servant leader requires that we adjust our skills (sometimes learn new skills) to help us really make the connection with followers that one needs to make to create a strong and trustworthy impression on followers that the leader is genuinely interested in being of help and service to followers.

There are many ways that we as leaders can improve those skills as we see in the next section.

Improve on your listening skills

Sometimes, we leaders (and upcoming leaders) tend to believe leadership is all about calling the shots. No matter how impressive the concept of bossing people around might seem at any moment, one should steer clear of this mindset and realize that the best leaders seek to understand the needs of their followers and hence seek to be careful listeners.

A listening leader balances the company's employees, and their interests ideally by actively listening to the employee's ideas and comments, regularly requesting feedback, and working towards their input to deliver non-biased service to almost everyone.

A perfect example of a leader who listened and was exceptionally successful in her time is Indra Nooyi, a former CEO at Pepsi. According to Read, Nooyi was entrusted with around 840,000 employees, and as a leader who believed unconditionally in the listening strategy, she led the team successfully (2020).

Listening acts as a sign that you respect your followers and do not take them for granted. While working as a delegate in the National Congress, I learned that respect goes both ways. One cannot gain respect from followers without first illustrating that you respect them.

Simply because of my determination to listen to my followers, I garnered their trust, and my followers approved any decision I decided to make. I had created a stable connection with them.

Upon mastering your listening skills, you will find connecting with followers substantially expedited.

Assigning tasks reflectively and recognizing the followers.

Sharing your ideas and goals for the company to the employees and the followers is essential and segregates a healthy working environment from an unhealthy one.

While assigning tasks, it is important to keep in mind that the employee responds better when they understand the overall significance of their contributions. When followers know the leader's aims and goals, they feel connected to the goals and the leader. The connection is further enhanced when recognition, specific recognition for work well done, is given.

Repetition works in favor of the leader when he/she states the contribution the followers will make upon completing the task assigned and when he/she mentions the impact completing the task had on the organization.

The president of the Union had mastered this trait, and it worked flawlessly for him. One instance etched in my memory is when he gave recognition in a speech for a completed task. Being among the task force, I experienced the powerful impact of recognition first-hand. The mood in the room changed, and I could feel the connection between us strengthen.

I went on to try out the strategy with my followers, and it did not fail. The act of delegating and recognizing thoughtfully and clearly impacts significantly on the connection between leader and follower.

Invest in your employees/followers.

Providing numerous opportunities for your followers to grow professionally and personally creates an important bond between you and your followers.

From such a bond, it is easier to create a connection. The opportunities can range from providing leadership training, issuing material benefits to skill management training. This will prove beneficial in that your connection to your followers will be improved, and the followers will be easier to guide since they have expanded skills.

However, investing in your employees does not have to be fixated on material benefits or training sessions. Spending quality time with your followers inside and outside the workplace is also a method that works. Investing your time to find out your employee's additional skills, abilities, and enthusiasm for certain interests establishes a connection between the leader and the employee since they strongly feel your genuine interest in them.

Understanding the abilities and values that employees bring to the organization helps the leader connect the followers better, leading to a connected workplace that guarantees more effective workflow and productivity.

Establish trust

Just like respect, trust goes both ways. You have to show trust to gain it. Having employees/followers you trust and who trust you is proof of a workplace with good connections and the potential for excellent performance all round.

However, establishing trust is not easy. It requires dedication and many sacrifices from both participants - the leader and the follower.

There are three very effective ways to build trust that leaders should be aware of:

- **Involve your followers in crucial decision-making**
- **Be honest in all dealings**
- **Ensure transparency and accuracy in communication and actions.**

Most leaders find it challenging to involve their followers in crucial decision-making because they are not sure of the follower category the employee is in.

For example, entrusting a pivotal task to an antagonist or a renegade could turn out the worst or the best decision for a leader since there are two very possible outcomes: it could lead to a very strong connection with either of those follower types or it could lead to the leader's downfall because the person performs the task in a shoddy manner, which reflects negatively on the leader.

For this reason, delegation of tasks must be managed by the leader (whatever the follower type) to ensure that trust is not being taken advantage of. Again, knowing your followers is important to being able to trust them.

Either way, the reality is that establishing trust is essential in creating strong connections between leader and followers.

Show interest in their personal life

A method that proves effective in forming close connections with followers is first creating personal connections with those followers, getting to know some personal facts about their beings and their lives.

Before being tasked with the leadership role in the National Congress, I used to wonder why leaders take their extra time to ask questions like "How is everyone doing at home?" or questions about the about the weather and so on; in other words, generally inquiring about the person's life.

But then it dawned on me that many many meaningful and potentially important relationships could be created by socializing. By bonding with a few colleagues, I secured important followers who aided in my reassigning to the team.

Socializing with your followers even outside work serves as an acknowledgment that your followers are not just followers but human beings with things going on in their lives, just like yourself.

Joining in on an occasional coffee break, participating in sport team activities at work, or sitting with a few followers for a chat during your free time, and genuinely being interested in their personal lives definitely can prove beneficial to connecting since it will create a sense of engagement.

Though the tips above might be considered strenuous to some leaders, there is no doubt whatsoever that connecting with one's followers in all sorts of ways and at all sorts of levels can significantly improve relationships, loyalty and understanding.

When a leader creates a stable and robust connection with his/her followers, the leader can reap the benefits.

Importance of creating a connection with your followers

A connection guarantees that both the leader and followers are in sync regarding the organization's aims and goals. Managing and directing a disconnected working environment is among the most difficult things a leader can be tasked to perform. Upon establishing a connection, the leader informs the follower of the company's mission. They can work in unison toward the goals and objectives, thus ensuring a smoother, more effective workflow.

The connection allows the leader to trust in the employee's ability to assume responsibility. When a leader establishes a robust and secure connection with the followers and finds out the follower's abilities and passions, he/she allocates tasks better according to the abilities and the areas of enthusiasm.

The leader can gauge the follower's level of personal responsibility to the organization and be sure that the follower is working toward the company/organization's mission. A self-motivated employee makes the leader's work significantly more manageable.

A connection provides freedom to provide feedback and ideas. A good leader-follower relationship is vital in ensuring a productive working environment where followers actively participate in the organization's goals. When this is seen to be working it can almost guarantee success and, in the process, bring fame to the leader. This is because the follower will add to the leader's ideas and potentially provide feedback in a situation where the leader might steer away from the organization's goals.

Creating a leader-employee connection leads to happier, increasingly engaged, and loyal followers. Trust, respect, and loyalty are the key aspects of a healthy working environment.

Achievement of these aspects is incredibly difficult in an environment with no connection between the leader and the followers.

A connection presents a sense of togetherness that proves essential to fostering collaboration, teamwork, and follower innovation, leading to followers who are dedicated to doing their best. In addition, the mood in the workplace will remain happy since the key to happiness at work (as has been said by so many workplace productivity experts) resides in building friendships and connections with workmates.

Summary

- Every leader has a group of followers whom he/she must understand before setting up a connection

- The Followers should not be looked at or considered as one joint entity. There are different types of followers, all with unique needs that need to be met to establish a connection.

- Connecting with followers can be enhanced by choosing a neutral leadership strategy for all your followers, embracing servant leadership, listening to your followers, delegating and recognizing work well done, investing in your employees, showing interest in the follower's personal lives, and building trust.

- Connecting with employees is beneficial to the leaders, and every leader should invest time and resources to learn about connecting with his or her followers.

CHAPTER SIX

FOCUS ON THE VISION

We now turn our attention towards the importance of vision in leadership and the content in this chapter is formulated to help leaders and upcoming leaders to get a better understanding of the concept of vision. We are told that 'without vision, the people perish' and by thoroughly reading through the chapter, I hope and believe that information about leadership vision will seamlessly be passed on from my mind to yours. The chapter covers three points broadly:

- **Importance of a Vision**
- **Developing your Leadership Vision**
- **Developing your Vision Statement**

… and sets out to explain leadership vision, elaborate on the importance of having a vision as a leader, define a leadership vision statement, and guide the reader through formulating an effective vision statement for themselves.

The chapter vividly explains how to develop a leadership vision in the most effective way possible and provides tips on sustaining the acquired vision. In conclusion, I believe the chapter is momentous to every leader aspiring to break leadership limits to become the ultimate leader.

Focusing on the vision

Vision is pivotal to achieving ultimate leadership. Directing towards a vision is a critical function of a leader. It requires the leader to set up the directions for combined efforts in the organization's workforce to guarantee progress in an organization. Directing without having a vision for the organization is pointless and results in the leader and workforce running around in circles like a dog chasing its tail.

Therefore, having a vision for the organization is essential for effective workflow. A leader with no vision seldom adds value to the organization, but a leader who envisions greatness works tirelessly to achieve the vision. The importance of directing in leadership is seen via the definitions of leadership experts from the past to the present. In their book "Executive leadership," Jacobs and Jaques define leadership as a process of providing meaningful direction to ensure collective effort towards goals and enabling willing effort that can be disbursed to achieve the purpose (Jacobs & Jaques, 1991).

Therefore, to understand leadership, one must understand the direction-setting role a leader ought to possess to lead effectively.

Regardless of a leader's organizational level, one must have a vision. The vision should act as a guidance system to your followers.

The top-level managers and leaders should have a broad vision that can be translated into diverse organizational visions and strategies.

The middle-level leaders and managers should have a narrower vision span, and the low-level managers and leaders should have a more direct vision that can be passed on to their followers.

Consequently, for an organization to function satisfactorily, the most important thing is that the leader (at whatever level) should pitch his/her vision effectively to his/her followers. This way, the vision flow remains constant (without complications) and everyone has the same goal for the organization.

A leader's failure to elaborate their vision leads to a chaotic working environment. Upon formulating a vision, a leader should choose a strategy that correlates with the vision and persuade the followers to adopt and execute the plan to work toward the vision.

This chapter describes leadership vision and equips leaders with all the necessary information to help them master and sustain their vision.

1. Vision Definition

There is no universal definition for vision. With multiple writers and leadership experts coming up with unique definitions, it is not easy to choose one among the many that are universally accepted.

However, amongst all the verbiage, there are impressive definitions that do ample justice to the word. These can be found mainly in the writings of Gardner and Awamleh, Kirkpatrick and Locke and Kotter.

Gardner and Awamleh defined vision as a mental image that a leader brings to mind to depict an organization's highly desirable end state (Awamleh & Gardner, 1999). On the other hand, Kirkpatrick and Locke defined a vision as an ideological, moral, general transcendent idea representing shared values (Kirkpatrick et al., 1996).

In addition to Awamleh's and Kirkpatrick's definition, Kotter defined vision as a straightforward description of something in the future in terms of the essence of what it should become (Kotter, 1990).

Deriving from the definitions above, leadership vision is a negotiated reality that a leader develops to guide all the members and followers of an organization to ensure the organization's success. Leadership vision enhances the ability to focus on the vital aspects of an organization or individual. A leader with a vision attracts followers who share in the vision and influences organizational effectiveness by making the goals and objectives clearer to both the leader and the follower.

Vision, especially for those leaders who feel something is lacking in the way they lead, acts as a game-changer in leadership. A visionary leader is a key to any successful organization or establishment. Outlined in the next section are the importance and benefits of being a visionary leader.

Importance of leadership vision

Does being visionary have any benefits? What is the importance of having a vision as a leader? Vision in leadership has a whole lot of importance and no disadvantages.

A visionary leader provides a more precise strategic direction than a leader with no vision. With vision, a leader mentally envisions the goals of an organization and, in doing so, effectively lays out the organization's missions. With these in place, the leader can formulate strategic direction for the organization, which can then be explained to the followers leading to organizational effectiveness. Vision acts as a sensemaking tool for leaders that enhances strategic direction in an organization.

Another importance is that vision, and its contents, provide a framework for future reference for both the leader and follower. Deriving from the definition of leadership vision, it is clear that vision is a mental image that a leader has for an organization. Based on a leader's past, personal, and work-related experiences, he/she can formulate a responsible vision for the organization he/she is directing.

For instance, a leader fascinated with nature preservation and sustainable living may develop a vision that sees the organization using energy-saving energy sources to reduce its general carbon footprint. This vision acts as a skeleton/ framework of reference for any decision the organization is required to make.

Before making procurement decisions, the leader and his/her followers must compare the decision to the vision and only go on with the decision if it meets the framework of the vision.

In addition, vision provides the necessary enthusiasm and innovation in both leaders and followers. A visionary leader extracts goals from the vision. The goals help keep the task force motivated and inspired. The goals act as checkpoints for the greater goal while simultaneously acting as a source of wholehearted empowerment that motivates both leader and follower. With goals in place, the whole team is constantly motivated to keep going. This provides focus to the task force because they know what they are working towards.

Vision in leadership can also work as a failsafe. The vision guides the followers and the leader and ensures that they remain on the right path towards success. The way this works is, whenever the task force veers from the vision, it is possible to put in place measures to steer the whole work body back to the right path.

The fact that vision ties the superior goals to the subordinate ones allows for easier detection of minor mistakes that gradually develop into serious ones. Consequently, the vision prevents potential social and organizational crises before they even happen.

In summary, vision in leadership is vital to the success of an organization. It promotes leader and follower enthusiasm in achieving the company's missions, helps generate strategies, goals, and missions, and provides a framework of reference for both the leader and follower.

In addition, it acts as a failsafe that detects potential social and organizational crises in the workplace and the other importance's and benefits outlined above.

Leaders should develop a leadership vision to reap the benefits and achieve ultimate leadership skills. But, in reality, many leaders ask if it is possible to develop leadership vision skills? Is it too late for me to start cultivating vision?

The answer is no surprise. Yes, and no. It is possible to develop the skill from scratch, and no, it is never too late to learn and cultivate any skill. While growing up, every wise person I interacted with told me there is no end to learning. That no matter how long you spend in colleges and universities, the learning never ends. I failed to understand that back then, but later, I understood their words as I grew wise. The section that follows will equip you with the knowledge on how to develop your leadership vision.

Developing your leadership vision

During a survey I conducted a while back in the National Congress, I found out that vision is among the most crucial characteristics of a leader. Followers tend to believe and follow a leader who brings fresh ideas and solutions to the table. Every leader aspiring to be successful in their leadership post should develop a vision. This can be done by following the tips below.

1. **Meditate on what success would look like in the organization or firm you lead.**

The easiest way to practice vision is first to understand what success is in your organization. What you would like the organization to achieve? After understanding what success means in your organization, incorporate the ideas that run parallel to your personal and social preferences, then plan on what you will require in your journey to success and the challenges and complications you might encounter during the process.

Finally, incorporate all the ideas in your mind. The picture that develops is a vision for the organization. Practicing these is a guarantee to developing a solid vision.

2. Normalize recording your plans.

Think back to the time a powerful politician made his/her first move to acquire the leadership post. Did he/she have a manifesto to corroborate the powerful and moving speeches he/she gave at rallies? The probability of there being a manifesto is exceptionally high. The manifesto serves as a tool of showcasing vision, especially for politicians, primarily because it entails public declarations of the policies and aims in their minds.

There are a variety of ways an individual can record plans. Writing down the plans is the most effective and efficient method. However, a method that worked better for me was developing podcasts since it was less time-consuming.

Recording your plans for the organization is the first step in developing a vision. The action clarifies an individual's thoughts and enhances their ability to develop visions for the organization. In addition to clarifying one's thoughts and enhancing the ability to develop visions, writing down the plans (or recording them) simplifies the part where the leader pitches his/her visions to his/her followers.

3. Find out your follower's expectations.

Developing a vision is centred around the leader's/individual's expectations. Nonetheless, the mistake a majority of leaders make is not considering their follower's expectations. Considering follower expectations is vital in acquiring their loyalty and approval. A leader that disregards this fails in understanding a critical feature in leadership: a leader is nothing without his/her followers.

Learning the follower's expectations provides insight to a leader who listens. However, a leader has to be choosy in selecting the followers he/she considers expectations from. After assessing your followers, choose the ones who seem to possess high degrees of vision. Surrounding yourself with people who have high vision is a guarantee to achieving vision yourself. Therefore, considering a follower's expectations aids in the development of a leader's vision.

4. Attend conferences

Leadership conferences might appear to be a waste of time, but once an individual seriously considers them, they can prove to be practical and lifechanging.

In conferences, the speakers are almost always more experienced in their particular field than the rest of the attendees. And yet, individuals who have attended a lot of conferences before might have acquired the thought that a speaker is less experienced.

This thought is the enemy of learning and will always lead to the loss of vital information required in that individual's field of work. I once attended a leadership conference where one of the speakers looked simply too young to have the experience to provide a speech for leaders at my level. However, when he rose and delivered his speech, everyone in the conference hall was singularly impressed.

The fact that the world has different organizations all offering different insights and challenges to those directing them leads to different experiences for every leader. Attending conferences ensures that you may learn from the experiences of others.

Listening to other's experiences provides learning on their ideas and solutions and might trigger the listener's ideas. This will, in turn, help in developing your visions.

5. Think ahead

Building vision muscle requires an individual to stop thinking only in the moment but to project one's mind to the future – the focus needs to be on strategic planning and thinking of the future.

By developing a mission-oriented mindset, an individual will stop thinking about performing the actions. Instead, they think about the ramification of their actions. This is what being visionary means.

However, it is good to realise that developing a vision is not enough. A wise leader should know that the secret to consistent results is maintenance. Regular maintenance sessions are required to ensure the vision does not degrade. Updating the vision regularly is essential in ensuring it remains current to the changing times. Not only should you update the vision, but you should also relay the change to your followers to make them aware.

Finally, ensure you actively work towards the vision. This will help keep the vision alive throughout.

Creating a Vision Statement

Upon developing a stable leadership vision, the only task the leader is left with is to develop vision statements that have the power to move the followers.

The leadership vision statement will enhance the effectiveness of the vision by ensuring that the followers understand the leader's vision. They boost the attractiveness of the vision and create an aspect of accountability since the vision statement remains constant. The leader and the followers can track the progress and compare it with the vision statement.

Therefore, the creation of leadership vision statements is vital to a visionary leader.

This book aims to help you to define a leadership vision statement, outline the essentials of a good leadership vision statement, and venture further into leadership vision statements, ensuring that every leader is facilitated with all the necessary information regarding leadership vision statements, particularly after completion of the section below.

My Vision Statement

Below is a vision statement I made and followed through to the end:

Being a leader/representative of the Trade Union, I will make decisions after consulting with my followers. I will always listen to their demands and suggestions. I will filter out any limited options I receive to ensure that I make the most nuanced decisions. I will perform my duties responsibly, respectfully, reliably, and decently.

Leadership Vision Statement definition.

According to Lucas in his book "Anatomy of a Vision Statement," a leadership vision statement is a short, specific declaration of a leader's principles, opinions, and the grounds for the work that needs to be done (Lucas, 1998).

This makes it easier for the followers to understand their leader. The leadership vision statement communicates the leader's expectations for the organization and his/her work-related objectives and guidelines. Although a guideline for good leadership vision statements is that they should be short and precise, some leaders decide to make them more elaborate and include a strategic plan that outlines how they will meet their goals and objectives.

Before writing down a leadership statement, there are a few basic things one should consider.

The first thing a leader should do is think long and hard about the type of leader he/she is and what their beliefs, principles, and opinions are. There is no point in speeding up something that will be the foundation for your future operations. Taking time to meditate will prove its worth in the end when you meet your declarations.

The second thing is communication. The best leaders are always considerate of their followers. Interacting with your followers will often provide new insight into your business operations and will guide you in achieving goals and objectives. Using the information obtained to formulate a vision statement ensures it meets the fundamentals of vision statements.

Finally, the leader should refine his/her vision. Before coming up with the final vision statement, ensure you have a few drafts of the statement. It can take a few tries before coming up with the perfect vision statement.

The primary aim of vision statements for leaders is to communicate with the followers without necessarily having to verbally explain themselves.

In addition, vision statements should also inspire the leader and followers and meet some essentials to be effective. Outlined below are a few essentials a good leadership vision statement should possess.

1. **A good leadership vision statement must be aligned to the future**

While coming up with a vision statement, a leader must focus on the future. He/she must include his/her future goals. The vision statement should be written in the future tense. However, leaders must be aware of the activities and limitations happening in the present in order to compose a realistic leadership vision statement.

2. **A good leadership vision statement should be inspiring.**

A vision statement that is inconsiderate to the followers cannot inspire them. Consequently, the leader should consider the followers before composing a vision statement so that they are motivated to work effectively. Studies show that workers are inspired by leaders who provide easy solutions to challenges. Therefore, including a solution for a significant organizational challenge will enhance the inspiration achieved from your vision statement.

3. A good leadership vision statement should be clear

Try as much as possible not to complicate the vision statement. Followers should be able to understand your work-related personality right away after reading your vision statement. Therefore, leaders should summarize all their thoughts and present them in a straightforward manner.

4. A good leadership vision statement should be distinctive

Aim at producing a statement like no other. Being original in composing a vision statement is essential to avoid all the cliches that could manifest. A copied statement will not do the leader justice since what the leader believes in and what is understood from the statement do not align.

Include your natural values, beliefs, and strengths in your statement. This way, leaders can assure the followers of accomplishing their declarations, and when performing an accountability test, the odds of failing it are lowered.

5. A good leadership vision statement should point out the direction of business aspects.

The leader's decisions should be centered around his/her vision statement. If the leader declares to be fair with everyone, this aspect should reflect everyday acts ranging from human resources to procurement. The leader should not favour while making decisions.

6. A good leadership vision statement should be practical.

Practicability goes hand in hand with believability. While choosing a vision statement, ensure that everything included in the statement is achievable either in the short-term or the long term. Failure to compose a practical vision statement degrades the leader's accountability since the odds of the leader meeting their declaration become low or even undoable.

Focus on your vision to acquire ultimate leadership skills. Vision is the only thing keeping you from your life-long dream to become the most influential leader version of yourself.

Summary

- Achieving leadership vision is essential in achieving ultimate leadership.

- Leadership vision is a negotiated reality that a leader develops to guide all the members and followers of an organization to ensure the organization's success.

- Vision in leadership is vital to the success of an organization. It promotes leader and follower enthusiasm in achieving the company mission, helps in generating strategies, goals, and mission, provides a framework of reference for both the leader and follower. In addition, it acts as a failsafe that detects potential social and organizational crises in the workplace.

- Sustaining leadership vision is just as important as developing it. Failure to sustain the vision might lead to its degradation.

- Leadership vision statements are essential to visionary leaders since they communicate directly to the followers on reading them. Therefore, every leader should give thought to composing a personal vision statement.

CHAPTER SEVEN

UNCOVER YOUR WHY

Knowing your reasons for wanting to lead significantly helps to inform your actions and thoughts as a leader. This chapter is a complete guide to uncovering your why. It is formulated to ensure that every leader who reads through this book will gain the motivation to find out why he/she leads. I will take you through my journey into uncovering my why in detail to ensure that the information is practical and convenient to every leader type.

The chapter defines 'why,' outlines the most common mistakes and barriers in discovering a person's 'why,' shows how to find your 'why' and explains the importance of finding your 'why.' In addition, the writer will take you through tips that will help you put together an appropriate 'why' statement for yourself.

In conclusion, the chapter ensures that every individual finds his/her 'why' in the most effective way possible.

1. UNCOVER YOUR WHY

World-class author and entrepreneur James Clear wrote: "When the why is clear, the how is easy." Understanding the how is vital in everyone's day-to-day life. It acts as a guide to getting what an individual needs or wants. The 'Why' describes the aim of doing what you do and expands an individual's way of life.

To find out the primary reason for doing what leaders are dedicated to doing – ie lead – a leader must know what drives him/her, what guides his/her choices and decisions. Let us unpack what a 'why' is and the reasons for its importance to leaders.

What is a why?

A lot of individuals have the wrong perception of 'why' in their lives. In brief, 'why' is the thought about what you truly desire in life. It is an assertion of one's intentions for doing what he/she does and why he/she chooses his/her way of life, the reason behind an individual's goals: both long-term and short-term. Each individual striving to master self-awareness to succeed ought to find out both the long-term and short-term goals in their lives.

A leader should have an elaborate personal 'why' that clearly defines their values, motivations, passions, and strengths; after obtaining the personal 'why,' they are then able to derive their reason for leading. Leadership 'why' describes the choices an individual makes when in charge of a group of individuals. It should connect every decision the leader makes, from leadership style choice to organizational goal formulation.

The 'why' is a guide to a leader's every action. It defines the leader's sense of purpose. In simpler words, a leader's why is his/her calling in life, beliefs/opinions, the reference point in decision making; and this ought to reflect in the leader's mission statement and their vision of life and work.

2. Activity

Conduct a brief survey on your close friends. Find out why they do what they do.   It might come as a surprise that the friends you expect to know their 'why' do not have the slightest clue why they do what they do.

In a survey I conducted on my workmates, only 20% of the survey respondents seemed to be self-aware and have a valid 'why.'

Additionally, Carver, in his research about self-awareness, found out that only a few individuals (19%) can accurately describe themselves wholly even after being given 24 hours to think and meditate on the question (Carver, 2012). 81% of the individuals in Carver's research and 80% of those in my survey do not know the reason for doing what they do. This trend, though disturbing, is a harsh reality.

However, I am confident that (although you might find yourself lying in the 80% at the moment) after reading through this chapter and meditating on yourself, the odds of slipping into the minority group will be highly improved. Before we dive into guidance into discovering your why, allow me to take you through the common mistakes people make concerning their' why.'

3. The most common mistakes in the 'why.'

Before discovering my true purpose in life, I used to work primarily for the pay. I was fresh out of school, and I needed a job to sustain my way of life, pay bills, and acquire basic human needs. Originally, I was very choosy and could not settle for a job that did not meet my values, passions, strengths, and motivations, but, after searching for a job that was just perfect for me and failing terribly, I decided to settle for the job that had the highest pay. In doing so, I had to disregard my passions, values, and motivations completely.

This, as I discovered later, is the most common mistake hindering people from discovering and following their 'why' in life. With all the wrong reasons for working, I was among the individuals with the lowest self-awareness. I had no idea what my 'why' was. Consequently, my long-term and short-term goals were irrelevant.

Why do you do what you do? Why did you choose to become a leader? Below are the most common replies that might be wrong reflections of an individual's 'why':

- "I could not find any other thing to do at the moment, so I chose to do this."

- "I received an offer that was too good to turn down."

- "I needed the extra cash to get the things that I value."

- "I was forced into a career by something/someone."

- "Individual X is successful, and I want to be just like him. He did this, so I am doing it too."

- "To live up to someone else's dreams."

One could get as limitless replies from asking the "why question" as there are stars in the sky. However, if the reason you give does not make you feel complete, it is probably the wrong reason. An individual's 'why' completes him/her. It has the power to give meaning to the individual's every action and decision. If your 'why' is disconnected from certain aspects of your life, it probably is wrong.

Therefore, after meditating, an individual should keep immersed in his/her mind and evaluate if their "why" is connected to each aspect of their lives. If it is, then the why is valid to the individual.

4. How to evaluate if your 'why' is the best version for you

There are four main aspects a leader ought to consider while evaluating his/her why's connectivity. These are values, motivations, passions, and strengths.

Firstly, the reason and purpose of a leader's life should meet their ideal values. These can be referred to as personal values. These are the primary beliefs the leader has that guide his/her every action and choice. The leader should evaluate his/her leadership style, interaction with his/her followers, and code of conduct in the workplace and establish a connection. When he/she fails to link the aspects to his/her values, the 'why' might prove problematic and inefficient.

In addition, a leader's motivations should match the 'why.' The best way to find out if there is a match is to first come up with an elaborate 'why' statement. The statement should guide the leader to knowing what his/her primary motivation is. The leader should then look at the current goals, objectives, and missions he/she employs to meet the long-term and short-term goals. If and when the 'why' matches the leader's motivation, it probably is a fitting why for the individual.

 Similarly, if the 'why' matches with the leader's strengths and passions, it proves appropriate to the leader.   Although finding a 'why' that matches with all the four critical aspects of an individual might seem virtually impossible, achieving it is possible but challenging.

"My 'why' is to share my gift of effective leadership with the world. From a young age, I made primary decisions in peer groups and was delegated to lead groups. This was recurrent throughout my youth and continues to happen to date. Leading is my calling, and I do so with humility, empathy, respect, and full commitment. Leading correlates with my values, motivations, passions, and all my strengths."

Finding a 'why' that connects with all my four aspects was not easy. I went through a long and tiring process of self-discovery, often meditating for hours on end.

However, I finally achieved the ultimate 'why,' and nothing feels better. It is essential to have a 'why' that corresponds with all four aspects. However, if you are only beginning to discover yourself, finding one that connects with at least two or three aspects is a huge step in the right direction. Once you start making moves, you only get closer to the end goal, and before you know it, you will have developed a 'why' statement that resonates with all your values.

The section that follows comprises valuable information in finding one's 'why.' It breaks down my personal experience in finding my 'why' both in life and in leadership, and other valuable tips and tricks I picked up from colleagues and workmates.

How do I find my why?

This is the question you are most likely asking yourself while reading this.

Leaders are more than just individuals issuing orders. They are instruments of change in the world. This is so because, being a leader, one can guide, shape, and influence groups and crowds of other individuals.

Therefore, it is important that leaders should aim to be as effective as they can in inspiring change in the world. The world can only be a better place with quality leaders standing in the front lines, guiding their followers as best they can. Finding their 'why' is necessary for their journey, and here is how to obtain it.

As mentioned earlier in the book, I used to work towards goals, visions, objectives, and missions that were not my own. The factors that motivated me were all the wrong ones: money, fame, and following the steps of someone who had achieved success in the same field.

I began my life-changing journey by reading successful leaders, scholars, and influential blogs and articles. Here, I drew inspiration from their life stories, learned what they did to achieve what they had achieved, and noted down what they did wrong in their journeys so that I could recognize a situation if it happened to me as I pursued ultimate self-discovery.

While reading, I noted down the key points from the publications, picked out the points that made sense to me and ignored those that did not. I was left with an elaborate set of more personalized notes. Going through these notes thoroughly and meditating on my life, I made considerable progress in my journey to find out why I work. I tapped into my unconscious and conscious mind to find out what I valued most, both in my personal life and my work life:

Helping others and making as much a difference in the world as I can.

Upon realizing this, all I had to do was relate helping others to my work life and let it lead to all the primary and secondary decisions in my life.

Having a statement that guides you guarantees that you are always working towards the bigger dream. I embraced a habit of updating this little statement: Helping others and making as much a difference in the world as I can, and developed it into the powerful 'why' statement it is now. The process guaranteed that the' why' went along with my values, motivations, passions, and strengths.

If I did something that did not correlate with any of the four aspects, I would instantly change it and make the necessary adjustments in my 'why' statement. Within no time, I developed a 'why' that went along with all the four aspects, which correlated personally and worked.

Following my personal experience, I formulated the following steps that I believe can guide you and help expedite the process of uncovering your 'why'

- **Read books.**

Reading is one of the most efficient methods of learning ever invented. Humans have embraced the art of storing information in books that can be accessed both physically and online as soft copy documents. Reading books that have been written by more experienced, successful, or idealistic individuals acts as a guide that provides insight to the reader. This is essential in uncovering an individual's 'why' since it acts as an eye-opener and a source of inspiration

- **Take notes.**

Edmund Burke, a famous philosopher, once stated that reading without reflecting is like eating without digesting. While reading, one is expected to take notes of whatever he/she is reading. This enhances the reader's reflection of the publication's content and helps the reader make a personalized, summarized version of the book.

- **Find out what you value in life.**

Use the notes from the readings to meditate and tap into your inner self. Find out what you would like to achieve and what your passions, strengths, motivations, and values are. Next, think long and hard about what you value most in life by looking at exactly those four aspects of an individual: passion, strength, motivation, and values. This will be the key to developing your 'why.' A method I employed in finding out what I valued in life was asking myself why I valued the said thing. One should only be content with a choice if it correlates with your personal life and work life.

Engaging yourself in a few self-discovery questions could also help in finding out what you value most. Here are a few questions that could prove beneficial: What do I consider success to be? Where do my passions lie? If not for money, what would I work for? Where do I want to be in the future?

- **Work towards the thing you value most in life and update it regularly to fit your work and personal life.**

Coming up with the final copy of your 'why' is no easy feat, and individuals must re-visit and change the statements before reaching the most refined version of 'why'.

Following the steps above will enhance the uncovering of your 'why' experience and help you achieve it in the most effective way possible. However, there are additional tips and tricks to finding your 'why.' These are:

- Listen to feedback from colleagues and workmates.

- Find out the things people thank you for most

- Ask other's opinions

- Brainstorm what you would happily do for no pay.

In addition, being a leader requires you to think about what benefits you can bring to your followers. Therefore, while following the steps above, think not only about yourself but also about your followers. Identify a few things that run parallel to your values, motivations, strengths, and passions, and that can enhance other people's way of life. This will help you achieve ultimate leadership skills, boost your popularity with the followers, and lead to a happier, friendlier work environment.

This goes along with the fact that happier employees and followers lead to more effective workflow. Nothing makes a follower or employee happier than being led by a leader who has a vision for himself and the followers.

Developing a robust and working 'why' statement

Developing a statement goes through the same process as uncovering the 'why.' As a matter of fact, a wise individual should come to terms with the fact that one must develop the two simultaneously. This I learned from a colleague whom I would classify as highly self-actualized.

While working towards uncovering your 'why,' you should be writing down your progress, gradually changing the contents in the statement. In my journey, I started with only a single word: helping. I made amendments as I continued discovering more about myself and was finally left with the elaborate 'why' statement I have today.

Therefore, all you need to do is embrace the writing culture. Upon discovering a passion, value, or strength, you were unaware of previously, make sure to update your statement. The first thing you should do is point out the most prominent motivations in your life, followed by your strengths, weaknesses, and values.

Next, compare the motivations with your strengths and develop a rough copy of your why statement. The final step is amending the rough statement. While doing this, you will be pleased with the amount of progress that can be achieved by simple consistency.

Having a powerful 'why' statement and uncovering your 'why' has proven beneficial to me in more ways than one. As I came to learn, this trait goes for everyone who has discovered their 'why.' After conducting a few surveys on my workmates and friends and performing an analysis of my life before and after uncovering my 'why' I came up with a list of benefits for finding your 'why':

1. **Knowing your 'why' drives you closer to success**

A few years ago, a close friend explained the importance and benefits of an individual knowing their 'why.' In her explanation, she shared with me an analogy: The analogy of the aqua-phobic man. Here is how it goes. A man afraid of water might fail to dive into a swimming pool for various reasons, but with the right motivation he will work against his fear. Knowing your why guarantees following through with your plans to ensure you are successful in the end.

5. **Knowing your 'why' results in satisfaction in the workplace**

The 'why' goes along with your passions, strengths, values, and motivations. Working towards these generally results in satisfaction in the work that you do. This is so because when individuals are guided by

their 'why,' they work towards precise goals, missions, and objectives in the most effective way possible.

6. Knowing your 'why' results in a leader acquiring additional leadership skills

A leader who is not self-aware only leads his/her followers towards the darkness. He/she does not know what he/she wants in life. However, upon uncovering his/her 'why,' the leader works with his strengths, passions, motivations, and values. This ensures maximum efficiency in leadership, allowing for the acquisition of better skills and experiences.

7. Knowing your 'why' results in better relations with your workmates.

Knowing your 'why' and sharing it with your followers and workmates allows for a connection between the two. This connection allows for collective working towards the organization's goals, missions, and objectives. This and the fact that the leader focuses on his/her strengths ensures improved relationships in the workplace.

8. Knowing your 'why' allows for enhanced creativity.

Working within the range of values you believe in allows you to find the loopholes in most barriers by finding solutions you might not see if you were unaware of the essential aspects of your beliefs and values.

9. Knowing your 'why' creates more confidence in leadership.

Think back to a time where you were informing others about a subject you were coherent in. Working within your strengths creates a sense of confidence in what you are doing.

10. Knowing your 'why' leads to better decision-making.

Self-discovery is no walk in the park. In my journey to achieving self-discovery, I came across a few barriers that ate up my progress and time. Navigating through them was like taking a driving test blindfolded.

According to publications by scholars and experts, these barriers are common and occur to a significant percentage of individuals trying to achieve self-discovery. In your path to uncovering your 'why,' the barriers below are more likely to occur than not.

Nonetheless, this should not be a cause for alarm. The section below provides the knowledge necessary to combat the barriers. You will be aware of the barriers even before encountering them, giving you ample time to consider the solutions.

Common barriers to finding your 'why'

- **Time allocation.**

Uncovering an individual's 'why' requires active participation in the process. An individual is required to invest time in that process. I recall spending hours meditating and asking colleagues, friends, and workmates questions that were vital in finding out my most substantial aspects.

I remember almost giving up on the process because of how long it took. You might also feel tempted to give up because you either do not have the time to pursue the goal or think the process is taking too long. The best advice I can give you is: if you have not yet started working towards the goal, acknowledge that this is no easy feat and that it will take up a lot of your time. Be aware of that fact.

If you have already started, invest just a bit more time, and think of the benefits you can reap from uncovering your 'why.' It will all be completely worth it in the end.

- **Lack of motivation**

This is a common barrier to almost everything you venture into. Drawing motivation from something or someone is an effective method of working around the barrier. However, I am sure that you most likely have all the necessary motivation in your choice to read through the book.

- **Inadequate self-management skills**

We all can be guilty of procrastination and putting thing off to the last minute. It is entirely up to our individual selves to acknowledge these problems (awareness and acknowledgement is always the starting place to personal change) and ensure that we put goals in place to overcome our weaknesses.

- **Lack of support**

While I was growing up, my grandmother always told me that no man is an island. Everybody requires support to work towards his/her goals efficiently. In my journey, I went through a phase in my life where those who believed in me were just a handful. Nevertheless, the few individuals in place were my support system, and I am very grateful for their actions. You will require a support system in your journey. Lack of this will be a hindrance in uncovering your 'why.'

- **Focusing on the wrong things**

Lack of focus can be an enormous barrier to finding your 'why.' You might find yourself in a situation where you have pursued an element thinking it was your reason for life (why), but later realize it was entirely the wrong 'why.' This almost made me give up. However, if this occurs, maintaining your sanity is essential. Pressure on! Giving up is not an option in this journey. Persistence in what you venture into is the key to success

- **Not trusting the process.**

Trusting in something not yet seen is arduous. To go around this, you should consider finding a mentor to guide you in your journey. He/she will act as your light in the dark cave.

In conclusion, uncovering your 'why' is essential, especially when you are

in charge of more people. It will influence your choices, decisions, goals,

objectives, and more aspects of your life. It helps guarantee enthusiasm in

what you do. The journey might prove difficult at times, but it is all worth it in the end. Following a few steps and working around the barriers mentioned above will benefit venturing into the process.

Summary

- 'Why' is the thought about what you truly desire that corresponds with an individual's values, passions, motivations, and strengths.

- Reading books, taking notes, finding out what you value in life, and working towards your life values will help uncover your 'why.'

- While uncovering your 'why,' it is necessary to simultaneously compose a 'why' statement that will guide you in tracking changes and understanding your 'why' better.

- The 'why' statement is developed by adding more information to your primary value in life and is a personalized declaration of an individual's 'why.'

- Uncovering your 'why' is beneficial in your personal, work-life, and to your follower's and employee's lives.

BUILDING YOUR LIKEABILITY

This chapter is about building your likeability. It is formulated to ensure maximum benefit to every reader since it includes social likeability, likeability in the workplace, and likeability in leadership.

The details of the chapter include the definition of likeability, the importance of likeability, the pros and cons of being a likable leader, general likeability, likeability in the workplace, likeability in leadership, steps to developing likeability, essential tips and tricks into developing likeability, reasons for being an unlikeable leader, how to gauge your likeability in the workplace, and my own personal experiences of this topic while in leadership.

By the end of this chapter, the reader should be conversant with this subject. Moreover, if the reader is classified under the less likeable area, he/she should have, by the end of the chapter, the basics enabling him to reverse the negative trend. The chapter equips the readers with all the necessary information to build likeability.

Building your likeability

Although it is often overlooked, likeability is an essential aspect of leadership. Through my experience in leadership and during my research on effective leadership, I discovered this as a tool that could prove to be a game-change in leadership: LIKEABILITY.

At first, the thought of being a likable leader was foreign to me as I believed that a leader should be ruthless, seldom seen smiling. While growing up, all the leaders I had crossed paths with had a stone-cold expression on their faces, and one could rarely see them in a jovial mood.

However, after a few years, I noticed their free nature towards their followers. The ever-so-mean leaders were now showing their softer side. Benevolence, the art of appearing kind and well-meaning, is a tool that has grown common in leadership. This is because it adds to a leader's likeability.

George Washington, the first president of the United States of America, is the only leader known for not smiling. The reason behind his not smiling is rumoured to be because he did not have teeth.

Even though he did not smile, his benevolence ensured that he was likable. Therefore, it is evident that no leader out in the world desires to build unlikability. Instead, every leader, me included, looks forward to making positive reactions to his/her followers throughout their term.

However, simply wanting to be likeable is not enough. Leaders should actively work towards building likeability.

This is not as easy as one might think it is. It can only be achieved through purposeful working towards building this attribute and, very occasionally, it is achieved by simple good luck.

By reading this book's contents and following the content entailed within, individuals are assured of building likeability in the workplace to achieve ultimate leadership.

What is Likeability?

According to the Merriam-Webster dictionary, being likable is the possession of qualities that bring out approving regard, such as being agreeable and pleasant (Merriam-Webster, n.d.).

Likeability, therefore, is the property that leads to an individual being liked. Unlike popular belief, likeability not a trait that can be achieved only naturally or by a few among the bigger population. It is a trait that can in fact be achieved by anyone through learning and developing Emotional Intelligence (EQ) – knowing oneself and knowing others and how to connect with them.

Faking traits to achieve likeability is popular in both current and past times. However, building likeability is not a trait that can be partially achieved and people are quick to spot inauthenticity – in other words someone pretending to be likeable when in fact they don't really care about others.

Individuals need to practice the trait in their day-to-day lives first before seeing the permanent results in the workplace. Just as an individual goes up the chain to achieve leadership (from being an ordinary member of society to being a worker at an establishment, to being a leader with considerable amounts of followers) so, must he/she build likeability from the roots upward.

Building overall social likeability

An individual ought to practice initially the essential skills to achieve likeability in the long run. Cultivation of people skills begins from an individual's youth.

While growing up, I was not as social as my peers; however, whenever I was in a situation where I needed to use my people skills, I made utmost use of the time. Through practice, I grew to be more sociable. This trait (sociability) can be learned at any time in an individual's life, regardless of age or social situation.

An important issue concurrent with building likeability in society (and one we must be aware of) is the use of phones. Through phones, it is possible to ruin your perfect reputation in a few minutes or seconds.

Allow me to engage you in a simple activity. Think back to a time in your life where you were in an intense conversation with someone. The individual you are speaking with takes out his/her phone and scrolls through the phone aimlessly. What would be the first thought that comes to your mind?

I once was in this exact situation, and the first thought that came to mind was that I had either grown boring to the person I was speaking with or the person was just rude.

Avoiding temptations to use the phone while socially interacting helps you to focus on the person you are with and allows you to be drawn to something that is not work-related but relationship-building.

Nonetheless, phones are not the only bad thing that could interfere with social interaction. There are numerous factors that can lead to a negative social encounter.

These are: being bogus, judgmental, inconsistent, negative in terms of body language, disinterested. While socially interacting, aim to be always genuine, without hiding your true intentions.

Although the idea of a sixth human sense is controversial, it may be achieved by using the other senses to derive reason for something. In addition, judging others should be avoided at all costs. Although challenging, it is possible. Try keeping your judgment to yourself. Within no time, you will find that you no longer judge others.

It is important to be consistent in our day-to-day lives. If you are kind one day and unkind the next day, a sense of uncertainty is created in your audience. Consistency is the key to achieving trust, and being trustworthy is the key to achieving likeability.

Finally, even without words it is possible to know what people are thinking or how they are seeing us. Being aware of your own body language, practicing positive communication and being extraordinary is sure to attract likeability in your social circle.

All of this forms a stable foundation for personal likeability.

Likeability in the workplace

Once one has worked on creating firm and healthy social and personal likeability, an individual needs to extend these skills to the work-life. Practice the skills achieved in your social work in your work activities.

Firstly, give your all to work projects, ensuring you veer away from disinterest. Instead, strive to be extraordinary and totally engaged.

As I learned, this action might attract negative emotions in the workplace since not everyone likes an over-achiever. However, through consistency, even the workmates who do not appreciate your extraordinary traits will grow to understand that that is just how you do things. This will ensure that you attract positive emotions, which will lead to your being likable.

Portray your skill of genuineness in the workplace. Being lower in rank to someone does not mean that you should lay down your ethics, goals, objectives, and morals.

Upon issue of a task you are uncomfortable with, make your feelings clear instead of doing a task you are uncomfortable with. This ensures that you conduct business with the right oomph all the time. Like being an over-achiever, this can bring about negative emotions but, with time, your authenticity and resulting likeability in the workplace is sure to increase.

Furthermore, laying down a judgmental nature will ensure that you follow instructions without the unnecessary questioning of every action. This boosts an individual's likeability in the workplace since he/she is easier to work with.

Speaking truth is essential. It is proven that rumour mongers are the most unliked group in the workplace. Rumour mongering, alongside other passive-aggressive behaviors, are linked to adverse effects on employees and organizational performance (Kent et al., 2014). Rumour mongering emanates from the judgment of others and leads to mistrust and lack of respect.

Likeability in leadership

Following one step after the other is recommended and is the most effective way to achieve likeability as a leader. Although one might work on the social part of likeability before advancing to the next step in the likeability chain, it is possible to work on all three simultaneously.

Upon mastering and reflecting on the previous two steps of building likeability, leaders ought to follow the guidelines and reflect the learning outcomes on their leadership style.

Understanding that followers are human and have the right to believe in their morals, ethics, goals, and objectives is key to being a likable leader. A leader who understands that he/she leads individuals is more likely to accept diversity in his/her followers. This is a factor that contributes significantly to a leader's likeability. This type of leader does not issue rules blindly. Instead, he/she is mindful and considerate.

A less judgmental leader is more likeable than a judgmental one. This is broken down in the actions of the two types of leaders. The latter is less understanding and is more likely to stir negative emotions in his/her followers than the former.

Picture this: a leader who judges the followers and categorizes them before getting to know them and knowing their circumstances can create discord and unhappiness.

Suppose there is a follower or employee with severe difficulties in getting to work early, and the leader judges the employee and categorizes that person as lazy, with no attempt to understand the situation. This will obviously result in mixed reactions in both the leader and the employee leading to misunderstanding and reduced likeability.

While working for a company, I was privileged to work alongside a differently-abled colleague with multiple personality disorder, commonly known as dissociative identity disorder (DID). This mental health condition leads to more than one distinct personality controlling a person at different times.

This could lead to the loss of memory and severe depression. There came a time where a change in management was requisite, leading to a switch in managers. Unfortunately, the new manager was not as understanding as the previous one.

During one particularly stressful event in the workplace, the manager and the DID worker clashed, and the manager called the worker insane and threatened to fire him.

This created a very negative image for the manager amongst others and led to his demotion from leadership. Although he came to know of the worker's mental health condition, it came to his notice too late and his judgment led to an irreversible event in his life. Judging without the necessary information is wrong, and every leader should avoid it at all costs.

The guidelines outlined in the sections above are just the tip of the iceberg. Below, further information from the research and personal experiences during my service as a leader is included to help leaders develop this important commodity of likeability.

How to build likeability in leadership

In the modern era, leadership is not all about the smarts and the monetary value you bring to an organization as a worker for the organization or company.

Leadership has evolved to encompass both competency and social skills. Without having both, it is becoming more challenging to capture the leadership posts arising in the world. Achieving social skills is therefore becoming more necessary to individuals aspiring to be in leadership positions. The aim of hiring, delegating, and appointing people with adequate social skills is that they are likable and possess the skills to hold together organizations while ensuring maximum organizational cooperation, trust, and outcomes.

An individual who can deliver this and live up to the organization's goals and objectives is currently the prime candidate for leadership positions. This can be seen as a threat by both the aspiring leaders and the current ones, but it should not be a cause for alarm at all but rather an indication of how we need to grow and develop.

Acquiring these skills is not difficult. With the proper guidance, it is as easy as attending a leadership mentorship session. Below are the methods I learned and picked up while in leadership and through research that I conducted on this topic.

1. Smile more often.

Leaders should not be severe and grumpy, as popularly believed. Popularity in leadership is based on quite the contrary set of standards. Most successful leaders are known for their outgoing nature in life. Be free with your followers and employees. Smile as often as possible. However, be sure to know where to draw your lines. Smiling too much, especially when you are not expected to smile, might come out as fake or sadistic.

2. Know people by name

My most substantial weakness is remembering people by name. However, I was forced to work around this weakness upon realizing its impacts on humans. At one point in my life, I worked at the front office desk. One rule for working at the front office desk was always to introduce yourself, informing the guest or visitor of your name. In addition to that, one always had to have a name tag.

This led to the people I interacted with always mentioning me by name; hearing my name always triggered a positive emotion for me (even though they knew me simply from my name tag or my telling them). Calling people by their name sends a signal that you have gone to some trouble to know their name, care about them and are conscious of their existence. This is a vital tool to building likeability as a leader.

3. Be humble

Leaders, despite their power and influence, should do everything with humility. Followers and employees do not like a leader who boasts or acts with pride. The humble leader is followed for his/her competence and expertise while the proud one is followed falsely. To build on your likeability, avoid acting with pride. Instead, practice being humble.

4. Make time for your followers.

My experience in leadership was often hectic. With almost no time to spare, leaders often fail to interact with their followers or employees unless when directly or indirectly needing something from them.

This trait is toxic in the workplace and might lead to the impression that the leader's voice or presence could only mean favors, tasks, and work.

Followers' and employees' need and value time. Making time for your employees is necessary to create a solid bond between you and your employees. While making time might sound like a difficult task, after forming a habit, it is not. It might surprise you to know that just a few minutes with one or a group of your employees can affect your likeability positively.

While walking around the workplace, do not shy from saying hello to employees and make small conversation to find out how their day is going or if they have any feedback. While doing this, I was able to discover things I might be doing negatively before they developed into a problem. This led to a great reduction in general tension in the workplace.

5. Listen

The power of listening should not be overlooked. Listening is the one tool that differentiates an influential leader from the one that is not. Make a habit of listening, not passively but actively.

Listen and act towards the words of your followers after considering the options. This will ensure that your likeability in the workplace as a leader increases significantly. In addition, it will lead to a healthier, more productive workplace since you, your followers, and employees will all be working towards the same goals and objectives.

6. Acknowledge your mistakes

Leader or not, humans are human and will always make mistakes. Acknowledging one's mistakes, therefore, acts as a sign to show that you are not superior to your followers and that you too can make mistakes. After openly acknowledging your own mistakes, correcting your follower's and employees' mistakes is not seen as criticism but more as constructive feedback correction.

7. Show gratitude

Ensure that you show appreciation for work well done and that your followers know that you are thankful and that their hard work was not in vain.

Leaders can show gratitude to their followers in a few ways, including giving treats such as special lunches, showing respect, recognizing efforts even when things do not go exactly as planned, offering a simple 'thank you' for work and favors well done.

Following these seven guidelines will add significantly to your likeability.

Tips and Tricks to achieving likeability faster

Following the seven guidelines above will ensure you build your likeability. However, by paying attention to the following tips and tricks, your journey as a leader could be enhanced even further.

- Be genuinely interested in your follower's life

- Encourage others to talk

- Avoid arguments. Instead, keep quiet and listen.

- Include your followers in the decision making

- Create fun activities in the workplace. While you are working hard, ensure there are enough bits of fun in the same workplace

- Give incentives

- Arrange work-trips

- Be a leader and a mentor

- Be professional. Do not overstep your employee's and followers' boundaries. Let work remain work.

- When you preach water, drink it. Do not do the exact thing you are talking against to your followers.

- Be honest

- Remain focused. Pay attention to the task at hand.

- Know when to open up

- Think before talking

- Practice. Practice makes perfect.

- Learn from your mistakes.

Importance of being a likable leader

Being likable ensures that you do not miss out on opportunities. However, likeability in leadership does not only mean being likeable to your followers and employees. It also runs along the lines of being likeable to your equals and superiors.

A likeable individual is more likely to be invited to forums than a less likeable individual, thereby creating greater opportunities. In addition to ensuring you do not miss out on opportunities, likeability plays a vital role in customer relations.

Research shows that encounters where the customer considered the seller as likeable are more likely to develop into meaningful and profitable encounters in the future.

Considering that a leader gets to cross paths with employees, peers, suppliers, contractors, and superiors, being likeable is key to creating good relations between the leader and his/her business mates at many different levels. It ensures supplier, customer, and employee retention.

Being likeable creates a feeling of relatability with others. A likable leader is simply easier to relate to.

Likeability is achieved by practicing emotional intelligence. More often than not, individuals with high emotional intelligence can explain themselves more fluently and personally, therefore being more relatable since feelings and life goals are expressed in a way that people can understand and appreciate. Likeability adds to an individual being understood by others.

Finally, likeability ensures that you get feedback from your workmates. When you attract positive feelings in the workplace, people will open up to you more. This creates the right environment for the provision of feedback even though people might be apprehensive about receiving feedback.

When you are provided with negative feedback, you will know how to deal with it more effectively. If the feedback is positive, you can choose to retain your actions or enhance them even further.

During a test I conducted with my peers, I asked whether it is necessary to be a likable leader and why. It was interesting to note that some people do not value likeability. Some of my respondents were able to provide a few cons to being likable which we explore below under the pros and cons of being a likeable leader.

Pros and Cons of being a likeable leader.

Being likeable is sometimes seen as being too friendly or weak. This trait could lead to the likeable leader being misunderstood for being malleable.

The major con of achieving likeability is the potential loss of respect from colleagues, followers, and teammates. Many people mistake a likeable leader for being a people pleaser.

However, in reality, this is not true. Likeability has been seen to result in outstanding achievements and excellent results by managing individuals in a most human, respectful and effective way possible.

Of course, in reality, being completely likeable is impossible. Pleasing everyone is not possible. You might think that you are likeable and loveable to everyone, but there will always be someone who sees all the wrongs in your life instead of the positives.

The pros of being likeable are significant and are best learned or observed practically through being a likeable leader. However, I will outline a few among the many to help you discern the pros when you experience them. Likeability leads to effective communication. Being likeable ensures that people are ready to talk with you and you are ready to listen. This leads to the most effective communication in the workplace.

Moreover, likeability plays a vital role in an individual's influence on others. Being likeable means that you are relatable, and you have authentic and sincere reasons for building your likeability, especially in leadership.

This creates the right environment for people to believe in you, listen to you, and follow your goals, dreams, and objectives. Being likeable acts as a guarantee that your followers and employees believe in you and trust you, therefore cutting down on questions about work-related actions being acceptable.

Now that you are aware of likeability, how to achieve it, its importance, and the pros and cons associated with likeability, it is quite possible that your are asking yourself an important question:

How do I know if I am likeable or not? The section that follows will help you answer this question

Am I Likeable? How likable am I?

Measuring qualities and characteristics is a challenging task. Also, measuring qualities can give inaccurate results depending on how the measurement is carried out.

On looking into the matter, I came up with a method that I believe can yield accurate results on a person's likeability.

Subconsciously, humans can measure likeability by examining a few characteristics that likeable people would score high in. These are familiarity, friendliness, the ability of the individual to be non-judgmental, authenticity, positivity, and the amount of interest the individual attracts. These six characteristics are my six measures of likeability.

To determine whether you are likable to the bigger population or not, you can conduct this easy activity with a minimum of 20 random individuals.

These individuals must have encountered you and have spent quality time with you recently and in the recent past. Print out or write down the six measures of likeability with a rating scale of 1-5, with instructions being one is the lowest and five is the highest rating.

Distribute the paper without keeping a record to ensure that the answers are provided with anonymity, which would help ensure that the respondents are as truthful as possible. The final characteristic of the list should be overall likeability.

Find out how your respondents rate your overall likeability on a scale of 1-5. Tabulate the results and find the average of each, then add up the averages. Finally, compare the results obtained with the following scale:

Likeability scale

11. Remark	12. Score
13. Overly likeable	14. 30-25
15. Likeable	16. 24-10
17. Under-liked	18. 9-0

19.

The task results should act as a point of reference in your plans to either develop your likeability or put in place measures to maintain them. Only maintain them when the results point out to you being overly likeable. Do not take the results too personally if the results are not what you expected.

Likeability is a skill that can be developed, and, if the results are lower than you expected, instead of getting angry or grumpy about the results, you can aim to develop the skill more to score better next time.

Reasons for being unlikeable

In his article "Nine Things that make you unlikeable," Bradberry outlines nine factors that could lead to an individual being unlikeable (2018).

Bragging tops the list in the factors for unlikeability. Bradberry mentions that bragging while hiding behind the cover of self-deprecation can be seen right through and is a reason for developing the negative condition of unlikeability.

In addition, he mentions being overly serious, emotionally exploding, boasting by dropping big names, misusing your phone, gossiping, and being close-minded (Bradberry, 2018).

In addition to these, failing to follow the guidelines outlined will lead to your not achieving likeability.

Summary

In summary, this chapter is all about building your likeability. It entails critical information necessary to understand and develop individual likeability, likeability in the workplace, and as a leader.

Likeability, unlike popularly thought, is not a skill that only occurs naturally to a select few individuals. It can be achieved by anyone willing to work towards developing a more substantial emotional intelligence.

Likeability is the property that leads to an individual being considered likable. Likeability is a skill best learned from the bottom going up.

However, it can be cultivated simultaneously in the three levels of life in the workplace: social, worker, leader.

Building likeability is achievable by following guidelines, tips and tricks. Being likeable has its importance but also its pros, and cons. Finally, it is possible to measure an individual's likeability by conducting surveys with the people familiar with you.

CHAPTER NINE

WHOLE PERSON APROACH TO LEARNING

This chapter focuses on the whole approach to learning as a way of being a leader. A leader needs to be versatile and a self-learner. Leadership is changing and so are those being led. The followers, due to the fact that they also know some leadership synopses know and also try to follow a leader who understands what he/she is doing. The leader's skills or ability need to be seen and not only inferred. The followers are often leaders in other spheres, and are also looking for ways of improving their skills. If you have followers either by choice or by the fact that you have a position. It means you are a developer of other leaders. They look up to you. Continuous learning which encompasses a whole person approach to learning.

Whole person approach to learning includes the holistic needs of the person, the person as a whole, it means being congruent of the self, the desired self and the emotional self. This also includes the spiritual self. How we learn, how we relate to others and, crucially, how we relate to the world around us.

Self-directed learning implies independent learning, self-planned learning, autonomous learning and self-education. Knowles (1975) defines self-directed learning as a process in which individuals take the initiative without the help of others to determine their learning needs, set themselves their learning objectives, discover human and material learning resources, select and implement suitable learning strategies and assess the results of their efforts to learn.

Heutagogy as part and parcel of whole person approach. Heutagogy, otherwise known as **self-determined learning**, is a learner-centred instructional strategy that emphasizes the development of autonomy, capacity, and capability with the goal of producing learners who are well-prepared for the complexities of today's workplace. Organizations are currently looking for managers and leaders that are of a caliber that can face changes, culture shocks presented by the global economy. In a VUCA (volatile uncertainty complexity ambiguity) world, the burden of change and the ferociously competitive environment of current business life push an organisation to out-perform themselves more quickly than before, this in turn requires organizations to look beyond the qualifications that one has but also in addition consider the ability to self-learn and adapt. The ability to get one elected to a position of power will not guarantee achieving success or getting re-elected. The ability to learn and relearn will.

Learning Styles

Navigating the leadership roles, I came across the VRAK (visual read/write auditory kinesthetic) learning method. In the 1960s through tests like, Myers-Brigg Type Indicator, a learning theory was propagated. It posits that different students learn best when information is presented in a certain way. In 1992, Fleming and Mills suggested a new model of learning. The VRAK model is used to explain different ways students learn. If a student is a visual learner a verbal lecture alone might leave them feeling unsatisfied, confused and frustrated. This is one of the reasons some people do not retain information after a Lecture.

Visual Learner

Graphical presentation of information is the pleasure of visual leaners. Men are also visual when it comes to women. The visual learners thrive with clear pictures. They prefer graphs, arrows, charts, diagrams and symbols.

Auditory learner

This is sometimes aural learners. They would enjoy best when listening to information being presented to them vocally. These learners work best in group settings where vocal collaboration is present, and may enjoy reading allowed to themselves. I had left university after obtaining a Diploma in Computer Science. I was employed as a Medical Records Officer in a Hospital. Later I enrolled for a Bachelor's Degree in Human Resource Management. It was a time when I was serving as a Publicity Secretary of Botswana Civil Servants Association. There were frequent travels. To learn I had to record myself reading aloud. The drive across the country became a learning expedition as I played the notes. It's always pleasant to listen to your own voice. This is a great way of learning.

Reading and writing

These learners enjoy working with the written word. They enjoy written information. They succeed with worksheets, presentations, and other text heavy resources. They are good note takers and good when referring to text. Being a leader will require you to develop this skill. The notes you take become valuable in the future. In the labor movement court cases are the order of the day. It doesn't matter what gets spoken, but what gets recorded.

Kinesthetic learner

These are people who learn by taking a physical active role. Kinesthetic learners thrive and get engaging all their senses and when they are hands on. Reverse engineering projects are best done by kinesthetic learners. I would fail to put back the radio I stripped, so I was not that good as a kinesthetic leaner.

In voluntary organizations, your ability to speak can break and make you. Gatherings usually attract auditory learners. At one of the election congresses, the leadership of the union had decided to hand pick the secretary general and employ him fulltime. They succeeded and after a lengthy debate, the congregants shouted, we want to hear him speak, we want to hear him speak. He was given the mike at the end there were roars of applause.

Whole approach practices

The whole person leader would benefit from the below practices

Individualized Coaching

Most leaders hope to do whatever they think without the support of a coach or mentor. The journey of leadership is so intense that some of the routes you will transverse are not easy; a helping hand is required. There are times you will ask questions and no answer will come, you have to question even yourself and the decisions you have made in the past. A leader who is individually coached will be able to support others get coaching and support. The best champions in sports all have coaches. We all know if they succeed it is their individual effort that is praised but if they do not win, the blame is shifted to the coach. Leaders need several coaches with different skills. There are leaders who look successful but end up being brought down by lack of their handling of person finances. Some are brought down by immorality and some later become paupers while they lived bountifully. A good leader is the one who is able to lead themselves. According to John Maxwell it is difficult to lead oneself as one has to walk the talk.

Funding for self-directed learning

It is imperative that you have sufficient funds to educate yourself. I was elected as a publicity secretary for an organization which had 20 000 members at the time. We were to oversee the operations of the organization at strategic level. We had to deal with stakeholders who pre-judged us as trouble makers or ungrateful people. One day a radio caller said that trade unions do not help people get jobs, but when someone gets a job, they start turning him against the employer. Training levy payers usually has refund from the training levy. It is common knowledge that those who think education is expensive should try ignorance

Purpose over Profit

The essence of purpose over profit is creating a business Model as an answer to social challenges. Purpose driven organizations have a competitive advantage and are creating better results over those organizations that purely focus on financial profits. Stimulating long lasting, sustainable value and positive impact is the new profit to be made. A leader who focuses more on purpose would be more successful. Individuals who focus on their purpose to serve over the ability of the opportunity of reward. I refined my strategy development skills as a volunteer at the hospital strategic committee. A lot of insight was also gained by assisting what they used to call improvement teams with the computer skills needed in their projects. It's always fulfilling to see people succeed because of your effort.

Develop a supportive Culture

Organizational culture is an integral part of business. It affects nearly every aspect of a company. From recruiting top talent to improving employee satisfaction, it's the backbone of a happy workforce. Without a positive corporate culture, many employees will struggle to find the real value in their work, and this leads to a variety of negative consequences for your bottom line.

According to research by Deloitte, 94% of executives and 88% of employees believe a distinct corporate culture is important to a business' success. Deloitte's survey also found that there is a strong correlation between employees who claim to feel happy and valued at work and those who say their company has a strong culture.

There's a reason why companies who are named as a *Best Place to Work* see so much success. These organizations tend to have strong, positive corporate cultures that help employees feel and perform their best at work. Research gathered found that employee's overall ratings of their company's qualities – including collaboration, environment and values – are rated 20% higher at companies that exhibit strong culture. Its only when employees feel happy that they will take responsibility for their development.

The leader should develop a culture where everyone is able to thrive equally. There are always inherent conflicts where some individuals are favored more than others. Never accept the 'scratch my back I will scratch yours' attitude. A supportive culture will provide the needed support for growth. A seed which falls on a supportive culture ground will grow and reproduce more seeds. The circle then will continue.

Define organizational and person goals and clarity

There were times when office bearers would be confronted by members wanting to know the role they would play in the organizations. In the Union we would name a few positions, but some will not see any fit. The Botswana National Productivity centre had developed some facilitators for strategy and planning. We engaged one of the facilitators and a strategy was developed. The vision was so clear that members identified with it. The organizational goals were so clear that members could see themselves in the organization. The clarity of the goals makes them perform better and grow other leaders. The union constitution was reviewed to align with the vision, and the hierarchical structure was clearly defined.

The leader also needs to have his/her personal strategy. If the leader knows where he is going, he will immediately know if the path of the organization and his/her path are in congruence.

Attend your Mental and spiritual health

What do you believe in as a leader? Are you in the right state of mind? When you medically check-up do you attend also to your mental and spiritual health. Spiritual health includes purpose, transcendence and actualizations of different dimensions and capabilities of human beings. Spiritual health creates a balance between the physical and social aspects of life. Spiritual health creates peace

In summary the approach to education and self-learning should be individual driven. There is a saying that when the student is ready the teacher will appear. The student directs and controls the learning. The student is being a leader.

DEVELOP INTUITION TO IMPROVE YOUR DECISION MAKING

INTRODUCTION

This chapter focuses on the development of intuition. Intuition is the cognitive ability of reaching a particular decision without reasoning. The ability to access the subconscious inner sensing, and gaining insight into some patterns and the ability to understand something with ease, without conscious reasoning or thinking. Intuition can be thought of as insight that arises spontaneously without conscious reasoning. The bible mentions something listening to a small still voice, and that voice providing guidance to the leader.

Intuition is not logical. It is not the result of a set of considered steps that can be shared or explained. Instead, while based on deep-seated knowledge, the process feels natural, almost instinctual.

And yet, while intuition is quick and usually beneficial, it is not always entirely accurate. The subconscious brain attempts to recognize, process, and use patterns of thinking based on prior experience and a best guess.

Something just doesn't feel...right.

You can't quite put your finger on it, but if life were a literal cartoon, little red flags would be popping up everywhere.

Maybe it's the "hmm" you thought after the weird way a first date ended or the feeling you get when you go into work on a Monday, questioning whether you should do this task or that task first. Or, maybe it's as simple as that thought bubble that arises when you reach a street corner, and part of you says to go left when you always go right.

All those little signs are your intuition.

Intuition is that sense of knowing what the right answer or decision is before you make it. It's a deep, internal, visceral feeling. You know your intuition is around when you say things like, "I can't really explain it, but..." or "It just felt right" or, more likely, "It just felt wrong."

What is Intuition?

Intuition "is the ability to understand something instinctively, without the need for conscious reasoning"

- Intuition is the way the subconscious mind communicates with the conscious mind. The information that informs 'that feeling' is real. It's like any other decision but the workings of it – the collection, the storage, the putting together – happen outside of our conscious mind.

- Intuition is your inner voice and knowledge within, without the influence of outside sources. People who are said to be "in tune" with their intuition might mean they are good at minimizing distractions and knowing what they want in life. For example, have you ever had that feeling when you walk into a room and just get a 'feeling' about something, somebody or the place in general? That's your intuition or your gut instinct. You know the feeling, when you just know instantly whether the vibe in the room is friendly or unfriendly, or if there's somebody who is particularly shy over in a corner if there are people arguing, even if you can't see it, seeing what's being said.

- Intuition exists in all of us, whether we acknowledge it or not. The more we can learn about it, the more we can use it to shape our lives for the better.

Is Intuition Important to leaders?

In a word, YES. Here are some ways in which intuition is important to leaders:

1. Intuition keeps leaders aligned

Deep down, we all know when something is "off."

But it's easy to ignore that gut feeling when our mind tells us that something is the "better" choice. Rationality can tell you that a deal, opportunity, or relationship is good for you. When deep down, we know it's not.

2. You can speed up response time

In a world where everyone is time-poor, speeding up decisions can be a superpower. Studies have shown that leading with intuition speeds up your response time.

This alone isn't that impressive, so it's good news that the same study found that "nonconscious emotional information can boost accuracy and confidence." You heard that right. Leading with intuition makes you quicker and more accurate.

Intuition helps Leaders survive by providing fast responses that, usually, offer an appropriate, immediate action to address a situation. Such responses rely heavily on "cultural capital," learnings specific to the environment in which Leaders find themselves.

While this usually helps Leaders, it can lead to bias and prejudice in our decision making – based on religion, culture, social, moral, and even political environments – and may need to be countered by rational thinking. The best results tend to come when intuition complements the hard evidence.

3. You'll become a better leader

When you go with your gut, the decision-making process becomes a lot clearer. You'll be able to stop second guessing your choices and give better direction to your followers.

Ways to develop your Intuition as a leader

So intuition is a brilliant thing. The sharper it is, the better off you'll be. Here's how to develop yours:

1. Shhh. Listen.

It's sounds simple enough – and it is. No tricks here. Your intuition can't talk to you if you're not listening. When you start to take notice, good things will happen. Just try it and see.

2. Trust your gut feeling.

When a word like 'gut' teams up with a word like 'feeling', you know there has to be a good reason. And there is. Research suggests that emotion and intuition have a physical presence in our gut. The gut is lined with a network of neurons and is often referred to as the 'second brain.' It's known as the enteric nervous system (ENS) and it contains about 100 million neurons, which is more than the spinal chord and peripheral nervous system but less than the brain. This is why we get 'sick' about having to make a tough decision or knowing we've made a bad one.

3. Feel

You'll know your intuition is there because you'll be able to feel it – if you let yourself. You'll feel it in your belly and it will goosebump your skin, send a shiver down your spine, race your heart and quicken your breath. Sometimes it's even more subtle and the only way to describe it as a 'knowing'. You'll feel when something is right – it will feel clear, nourishing and enriching.

And you'll feel when something is off – for me it's an ache or a flattening. Trusting your intuition might be difficult at first if you're not used to it, but give it time and trust it bit by bit, if that feels better. It will be worth it.

4. Be ready to let bad feelings go.

Negative emotions wil cloud intuition, which is why when you're angry or depressed bad decisions can happen so easily. Research has backed this, finding that people made better intuitive choices in a task when they were in a positive mood as compared to when they were in a negative mood.

5. Be deliberate about the people you hang on to.

People who drain you will add to the noise and make it more difficult to hear what your intuition wants you to hear. Chances are that you already know how things are. If not, be still for a moment – your intuition will be trying to tell you. Keep people who enrich and empower you and walk away from those who drain you. Understandably, you can't always walk away from the troublesome ones and if that's the case, empower yourself by making it *your* decision to stay, rather than theirs so that they don't take away your choice. The difference is subtle in language but big in impact. One lets the power stay with you, the other gives it over to them.

6. Pay attention to what's going on around you.

The more information you are able to gather from the environment, the more the intuitive, subconscious part of your brain has to work with – and the more accurately it will inform your decisions.

7.   Connect with others.

There are so many things that inform our opinions and decisions other than speech. Tone, volume of speech, body language, gestures – they all contribute to the meaning we give to our interactions with people. Sometimes, we have a feeling about people but can't quite put a finger on what it is. People might seem distant, distracted, uninterested, and often these aren't spoken but are 'picked up' in different ways. The ability to pick up on the thoughts, feelings, and intentions of others is referred to as 'empathic accuracy'. The more time we spend with people, the more we can finely tune or empathic accuracy. Being able to pick on the signals of others will all add to intuition.

8.   Find time to be silent and still.

Having solitude turns down the clamour of the world and allows you to tune in to your intuition. Our intuition is always sending warnings and encouragement but often we are too busy to notice. Let your mind wander and be open to what comes to you – feelings, thoughts or words. One of the ways to do this is through mindfulness. By focusing your thoughts on your own experience in the present moment, mindfulness gets rid of mental clutter and makes way for you to connect with your intuition.

9. Use your dream time well.

Dreams are the brain's way of processing information that's left over from the day. They are rich with valuable data – experiences, memories, learnings – so they can work hard if we let them. Paying attention to dreams can provide information that we may not have access due when we are awake. Before you fall asleep, turn your thoughts to any unresolved issues or problems. Think about possible options or resolutions as you're falling asleep. Close your eyes and let your brain do the rest.

Summary

It is important for a leader to develop intuition. Intuition is making the right decision without reasoning. It is important to leaders as it keeps leaders aligned. It improves their response time. It also helps leaders connect.

REFFERENCES

1. Read, W. (2020). *The Top 50 Listening Leaders.* Sideways6. Retrieved August 9, 2021. Retrieved from https://ideas.sideways6.com/article/the-top-50-listening-leaders Sendjaya, S., & Sarros, J. C. (2002).

2. Servant Leadership: Its Origin, Development, and application in Organizations. *Journal of Leadership & Organizational Studies, 9*(2)

3. Awamleh, R., & Gardner, W. L. (1999). Perceptions of leader charisma and effectiveness: The effects of vision content, delivery, and organizational performance. *The leadership quarterly, 10*(3), 345-373.

4. Jacobs, T. O., & Jaques, E. (1991). Executive leadership.

5. Kirkpatrick, S. A., Locke, E. A., & Latham, G. P. (1996). Implementing the vision: How is it done? *Polish Psychological Bulletin.*

6. Kotter, J. (1990). Management Vs. Leadership; «. *Work is a force for change.*

7. Lucas, J. R. (1998). Anatomy of a vision statement. *Management Review, 87*(2),

8. Carver, C. S. (2012). Self-awareness

9. Bradberry, T. (2018, January 3). *Nine Things That Make You Unlikable*. Forbes. https://www.forbes.com/sites/travisbradberry/2017/01/24/nine-things-that-make-you-unlikeable/?sh=2f938d18f74a

10. Kent, S., Troth, A. C., & Jordan, P. J. (2014). Mapping the terrain of aggression within the workplace context. In *Emotions and the organizational fabric*. Emerald Group Publishing Limited.

11. Merriam-Webster. (n.d.). Likable. In *Merriam-Webster.com dictionary*. Retrieved October 24, 2021, from https://www.merriam-webster.com/dictionary/likable

12. Cunningham, M. R., & Barbee, A. P. (2000). Social support.

13. Ell, K. (1984). Social networks, social support, and health status: A review. *Social Service Review*, *58*(1), 133-149.

14. Finfgeld-Connett, D. (2005). Clarification of social support. *Journal of nursing scholarship*, *37*(1), 4-9.

15. Merriam-Webster. (n.d.). Support. In *Merriam-Webster.com dictionary*. Retrieved October 24, 2021, from https://www.merriam-webster.com/dictionary/likable

ABOUT THE AUTHOR

I graduated and was posted to a Government Hospital to lead a Medical Records function. I did not have basics in terms of leadership skills. I know they always says leaders are born. I think they refer to royal Leaders who at times its claimed that their blood is blue. They also might be referring to political leaders.

How about those who are newly employed and they find out that they have to lead a team? Not all universities will offer a module in Leadership. I had to rely on positional power to lead the team. It was not always easy. I was later elected as a Publicity Secretary for Botswana Civil Servants Association. The span of my control now increased. I always had to argue my way out in all situations. I once scared potential voters by using unacceptable language.

I read every affordable book I could find on leadership. (Finances always limit what you can read). I still had to be chased away from Central Executive Committee meetings, when my views were not taken cognizance of. I thought to myself 'how do I position myself to make my views without risking being booted out by group thinkers?'. That's when I slowly developed my leadership skills. Some of the knowledge is captured in this book. And some others knowledge in books to follow.

Pambana Masame was born and bred in Moroka Village, Botswana. He holds a Doctorate in Management Studies, a Master's in Business administration, a Masters in Financial Management, A Bachelor's Degree in Information Technology, a Bachelors in Commerce in Human Resources and Industrial Relations.

He has worked as a Chief Medical Records Officer in a referral Hospital, a Trade Union regional organizer and as Human Resource Manager in a Financial services institution. He is a member of various professional organizations including Botswana Institute of Chartered Accountants, Professional Speakers Association of Southern Africa, and Toastmasters

He held leadership positions in workplace organizations and was instrumental in the transformation of an association into a fully-fledged trade union.

ISBN: 978 99968-63-50-9